Boy It's A Circus

by

Ray Warfel, Jr.

Truth
Publications

*Taking His hand,
Helping each other home.* ™

ISBN 10: 1-58427-243-0

ISBN 13: 978-158427-243-4

First Printing: 2008

Truth Publications, Inc.
CEI Bookstore
220 S. Marion St., Athens, AL 35611
855-492-6657
sales@truthpublications.com
www.truthbooks.com

Table of Contents

**Dedicated to
Raymond C. Warfel
(1932 – 2005)
The man I called Grandpa**

A Note of Thanks

If this is the first measure of my symphony of work, I want to thank a few who have been instrumental in it.

My parents, they tuned my ears to the harmony of truth.

My wife, she has patiently endured my banging at the keys.

My friend Steve Wolfgang, he encouraged me to take up the conductor's baton.

Preface

I am concerned for my son. I am concerned for my brother, and his son. I am concerned for the vast number of boys who will set their eyes on manhood in the next decade.

Our society mocks manliness. It encourages Bart Simpson to become his father Homer. Adding to this is the natural difficulty of growing up, going from boyhood to manhood. This change can be chaotic, crazy, a circus—thus the title.

Parents who are eager to help their sons navigate these years are sometimes at a loss to know where to start. *Boy It's a Circus* is a tool for these parents and their sons. This book is designed to give fathers a place to start a dialog with their sons about manhood. Questions at the end of each lesson reiterate the points made in the reading, and can be a good place to start talking.

I have tried to arrange the subjects in a logical progression—from a general to a specific. Lesson one is about manhood in general. Every lesson to follow then is on some specific facet of being a man. Then, since Christ ought to be first in our lives, becoming a Christian ought to be discussed as the first specific subject of being a man. Some lessons go together, and these also follow the general to specific formula. Lessons three and four go together, how to treat other people and then specifically friends. Lessons five and six likewise go together, dealing with anger and then specifically dealing with the tongue. Other lessons pair nicely too.

Whatever order you follow however, you will find that the Bible is the primary source of information in each lesson. This is because the Bible is central to all good men. Whatever other points may be taken from this book, I pray this one will go with every reader.

Finally, while this book is intended for a father and son, single mothers will find it especially helpful. Also with thirteen lessons this book is suitable for a Bible classes.

September 3, 2008
Ray Warfel, Jr

Introduction

Many Christians today have expressed concerns about the problems facing our young people. Especially is this true regarding young men, who are deemed "at risk" by some sociologists and others who claim expertise in studying such things. Such observations are commonplace, and by simply looking around one can discern ample reason for such concerns.

While many stand around wringing their hands over such problematic prospects, Ray Warfel decided to do something about it. You hold the result in your hands.

Ray is a diligent and caring father to his children, and in one sense this work is another of his "children." I have watched him "parent" it from birth to maturity, sweating and agonizing over the process of writing, revising, editing, and re-writing again to try to "get it right." It has grown up with nurture and love, as well as the occasional bouts of frustration and annoyance which accompany a maturing process.

In that process, Ray has learned – and is teaching – not only the significance of conceiving something, but the importance of persevering to bring it to completion. His willingness to seek advice and to listen to suggestions gives him standing to ask others to listen to his counsel and reflections. I have observed him develop and grow in many ways himself – in his own marriage, as a father to his children, and in his respectful relationship with own father.

Ray Warfel is cognizant of the contributions of past generations, not only as a student of history but also beyond academic pursuits. He is aware of and grateful for the sacrifices made by past generations so that we might enjoy privileges and benefits available to us today. As a result, he is concerned enough to see the torch of those blessings passed on to future generations. Keep reading and turning pages, and you will reap the benefits of Ray's acumen and wisdom.

Thanks, Ray – I commend both you and your work to a wide readership.

— Steve Wolfgang

The Greatest Show On Earth
Making Men

P. T. Barnum called his circus, *The Greatest Show on Earth*. This phrase is also a good description of the move to manhood. Physical changes, changes in interest, and many other changes can make us feel like a sideshow exhibit. There are critics too who do not see the honor and nobility of manhood. But in spite of these challenges it is still great to be a man.

God said, "Let Us make man in Our image, according to Our likeness . . . and God created man in His own image, in the image of God He created him" (Gen. 1:26-27). Two facts stem from these verses. First, God alone defines what a man is. And second, being a man is about being what God says a man is. In this lesson we will explore these facts and with them foster the confidence to become men.

Who Defines Man?

One woman I know diagnoses every act of stupidity, selfishness, and stubbornness as symptoms of *man disease*. Granted, some guys deserve a bad reputation. Some are selfish. Some are mean. Some are foolish. Somewhere some guy is still driving some worn out circle because he refuses to stop and ask for directions. However, the failings of some and the diagnosis of one woman do not define man.

Most television programming has the same attitude toward men. Homer Simpson could be the poster child for *man disease*. He is fat, bald, and one hundred IQ points dumber than his daughter. Still he is the safety supervisor for his town's nuclear power plant. But Homer Simpson is not a man. Simpson is a cartoon, and such shows do not define man.

Our father's generation cannot define man either. I respect my father, my elders, and I am sure they are men. They cannot though, define man. They cannot give or withhold permission to be a man. There is a guy who has nicknamed me Little Ray because my dad and I have the same name. I am as big as my dad. I have a wife, a job, and a mortgage. I have a son—Tiny Ray I suppose—but to this one man I will always be Little Ray. But I do not need his permission or acknowledgment as a man to be a man.

No opinion matters so much as God's because God alone defines what a man is. Before we get to God's definition though, let's look at His conclusion. What does God conclude about manhood? The Bible says, "God saw all that He had made, and behold, it was very good" (Gen. 1:31). God made man perfect. God made man just the way man should be made. So being a man, and acting like a man are good.

God's ability to make things the way they ought to be is seen in everything He has made. God made woman as a "helper suitable" for man (Gen. 2:20). God gave the Law of Moses to the children of Israel "for [their] good" (Deut. 10:13). The organization and independence of each local church also shows God's wisdom (1 Pet. 5:1).

> Men do not need fixing any more than women, God's law, or His church need fixing. Men need only to act as God defined them, and made them to act.

God made all things perfectly. None of God's work needs fixing. His work only needs to be diligently preserved. People make their lives miserable by tinkering with God's work. Feminists reject the role God made for women (Eph. 5:22; 1 Pet. 3:1-6), and are miserable. People reject purity before marriage, faithfulness afterwards (Heb. 13:4), and ruin their bodies with diseases and splinter their emotions. Religious people write creeds to promote unity and only bring about more denominational division. Men do not need fixing any more than women, God's law, or His church need fixing. Men need only to act as God defined them, and made them to act.

Men or Adult Males

When men do not behave as God made men to behave they confuse themselves, and the next generation about what a man is. We need to distinguish men as God made and named them from physically mature males.

God calls people what they are. God calls a woman who is joined to another man, while her husband is living, (Rom. 7:3) an adulteress, because she is an adulterous. Jesus calls those who serve God to be noticed by men hypocrites, because their actions are hypocritical (Matt. 6:1-18). God calls disciples who follow Christ, learn from Christ, and conform themselves to the image of Christ (Rom. 8:29) Christians (Acts 11:26), because they are like Christ. But God does not call people who act like animals men.

God said, "And I searched for a man among them who should build up the wall and stand in the gap before Me for the land, that I should not destroy it; but I found no one" (Eze. 22:30). What was God looking for when He searched for a man? Was God searching for someone to exploit women? The land was full of fornication, but God failed to find a man (Ezek. 22:9-11). Was God looking for someone to fight, cuss, or raise Cain? There was plenty of violence too (Ezek. 22:29), but still God could not find a man.

God was looking for someone who would conduct himself as God ordered. God was looking for someone who would stand up against violence. God was searching for someone to build a wall, defend virtue, and protect the weak. God was looking for a man but no man could be found.

How sad that statement is. I memorized verse thirty as a boy and determined that God would not seek in vain again. I am writing this book for that reason. I need to be reminded of what a man is. And I want to help you discover God's will too. I want to persuade you that God's will is worth following. I want you too to be a man, to be a man God can count on.

Men of Action

The Bible says, "But prove yourselves doers of the word, and not merely hearers who delude themselves. For if anyone is a hearer of the word and not a doer, he is like a man who looks at his natural face in a mirror; for once he has looked at himself and gone away, he has immediately forgotten what kind of person he was. But one who looks intently at the perfect law, the law of liberty, and abides by it, not having become a forgetful hearer but an effectual doer, this man shall be blessed in what he does" (James 1:22-25).

The Bible says in another place, "Be diligent to present yourself approved to God as a workman who does not need to be ashamed, handling accurately the word of truth" (2 Tim. 2:15). The right and accurate way to handle truth is to apply it.

Knowing what a man is, what God says a man is, is good – but it is not enough. Knowledge must be applied. Jesus illustrated this point at the end of His Sermon on the Mount (Matt. 7:24-27). Jesus told of two men. One man was wise, and the other was not. Each man built a house. Each house faced a storm. One house withstood the storm, but the other was destroyed by it. The difference between the wise man and the fool is action. Both the wise man and the fool had the same information. The wise man however, applied the knowledge and acted accordingly, but the fool closed the book.

Conclusion

The move into manhood can be crazy—boy it's a circus. It can be difficult to even determine what a man is for all the opinions around. But listen to God's word and follow it because it is great to be a man.

Questions

Short answer

1. In whose image is man created? _____

2. Why can the failing of some guys and the opinions of others not define man? _____

3. Give some examples of manhood in television and movies. _____
_____
_____

4. Why does God conclude that man is good even though many guys do bad things? _____
_____

5. What happens when people try to fix what God has made? _____
_____

6. Why could God not find a man among His people? _____
_____

7. How are we to accurately handle the word of truth concerning manhood? __
_____

8. What distinction does Jesus make between the wise and foolish man? _____
_____

9. Why is it great to be a man? _____
_____

10. When do you think boys become men? _____
_____

True or False

_____ 1. Real men behave like God made men to behave.

_____ 2. *Man disease* would be cured with an injection of estrogen.

_____ 3. God names people according to their deeds.

_____ 4. There were no males in Israel when God sought for a man.

_____ 5. Becoming a man will only take time.

Thought Question

What are some physical changes, changes in interest, and other changes that boys experience as they develop? _____
_____

The Man on the Flying Trapeze
Becoming a Christian

What makes the man on the flying trapeze so brave? Is it his strength? He is strong, but many can hold the trapeze bar. Is it his timing? He has good timing, but this is not rare either. It is his partner. The trapeze artist can let go of the bar because he trusts his partner to catch him.

A Christian can walk through life with confidence because he knows Jesus will save him (Heb. 11:6). The man who rejects Jesus though, is like the trapeze artist who lets go of the trapeze and refuses his catcher's outstretched hands.

In this lesson we will consider several reasons to become a strong committed Christian. We will consider what God has told us to do to become Christians. You may also find, after thinking about this lesson, that you are ready to obey Him.

Benefits of Being a Christian

Jesus offers His disciples several blessings. Paul enumerates many of these in his letter to the Ephesians. He starts the list saying, "Blessed be the God and Father of our Lord Jesus Christ, who has blessed us with every spiritual blessing in the heavenly places in Christ" (Eph. 1:3).

The key to these spiritual blessings is the phrase "in Christ." We will talk more about this in a moment. First however, let's think about these blessings.

Adoption. Redemption. Inheritance. Many of the blessings Paul lists, like these just mentioned, center on salvation. Each of these, of course, has an individual meaning, but in general the blessing Christians have is salvation. In another place Paul wrote, "It was for freedom that Christ set us free" (Gal. 5:1). And Jesus himself said, "You shall know the truth, and the truth shall make you free" (John 8:32). The freedom that these verses deal with is freedom from sin, and sin's consequences.

Sin has always been the agent of death. James wrote, "when sin is accomplished, it brings for death" (James 1:15). Adam and Eve were the first to find this out. God told Adam and Eve, "in the day that you eat from it you shall surely die" (Gen. 2:17). The day they ate of the forbidden tree they did die. God removed them from His garden and fellowship. God separated Himself from them, and that is death.

Fortunately for us God wrote more than three chapters of Genesis. The Bible says about Jesus, "In him was life" (John 1:4). Just as Jesus created all things in the beginning Jesus recreates spiritual life now.

There are other blessings that Christians enjoy. Being "born again to a living hope" (1 Pet. 1:3) is one.

Most boys do not spend their time pondering the permanence of death. As boys, my friends and I spent many afternoons playing army. No matter what happened on those backyard battlefields by supper every combatant was able to get up and run home. Death meant nothing more than "I got you" and lasted only as long.

Sometimes though, the real nature of death breaks into our lives. A grandparent dies. A friend, or a sibling does. In these tragedies though Christians are blessed. The apostle Paul said, "we do not want you to be uninformed, brethren, about those who are asleep, that you may not grieve, as do the rest who have no hope" (1 Thess. 4:13). We grieve when Christians die, but not like everyone else. Christians say good-bye only for a time. Those without Jesus do so forever.

Another blessing is God's providence. Every generation has trouble. My grandparents were born into the Great Depression. World War II was their childhood. After these troubles there was the Cold War and the threat of nuclear annihilation. What should we do when these kinds of troubles threaten? Worry that the worst may happen? Put our lives on hold dreading the future? No. We should be or become Christians. We should live our lives in the peace and knowledge that our God "rules in the kingdoms of men" (Dan. 4:17 NKJV).

A fourth blessing is God's guidance. Jeremiah the prophet said, "I know, O Lord, that a man's way is not in himself; nor is it in a man who walks to direct his steps" (Jer. 10:23). In the beginning of the chapter Jeremiah tells the people to, "Hear the word which the Lord speaks. . . . Do not learn the way of the nations" (Jer. 10:1-2). The nations trusted helpless idols (Jer. 10:5). But our God is not helpless. He helps. He guides. The wisest plan anyone can form is to hear God's word and let it guide him.

Boy It's a Circus

Becoming and Being
A Christian

We saw before that God put every spiritual blessing in Christ. To be blessed then, we need to be in Christ. We need to be added to Christ's body. The Bible states that people are, "baptized into Christ" (Rom. 6:3) and, "baptized into one body" (1 Cor. 12:13). Paul continues to describe this baptism as a burial (Rom. 6:4). An example of this "burial" (baptism) is recorded in Acts. "They both went down into the water, Philip as well as the eunuch; and he baptized him (Acts 8:38). Bible baptism is a burial in water.

Before we can be baptized however, we must believe that "Jesus Christ is the Son of God" (Acts 8:37). When Philip and the eunuch came to some water, the eunuch asked Philip, "What prevents me from being baptized? And Philip said, 'If you believe with all your heart you may'" (Acts 8:36-37). The eunuch did believe and told Philip so.

We must also repent of our sins. On the Jewish feast of Pentecost Peter told the crowd, "Repent, and let each of you be baptized in the name of Jesus Christ" (Acts 2:38). These same Jews had only days before demanded that Jesus be crucified (John 19:6). They rejected Jesus and His authority. Now they must accept Him. They must submit to His will. This is repentance. This is turning from sin and turning toward God.

When we are baptized like the eunuch or the penitent Jews of Pentecost we become Christians. We are added to Christ's body, the church (Acts 2:47; Eph. 1:22-23). Our sins are washed away (Acts 22:16).

Now we need to start acting like Christ. Going to the synagogue was part of Jesus' custom (Luke 4:16). Christians are faithful to attend worship services and they worship when in attendance (Acts 20:7; Heb. 10:25). Jesus loved his disciples (John 13:1). He may not have always liked the disciples. They may have irritated him at times, but Jesus always did what was best for the disciples. Christians love one another in this same way (John 13:34). Jesus made the good confession (1 Tim. 6:13). Before Pilate, Jesus confessed that He was king (John 18:37). Christians acknowledge the same. By what they say and do, Christians confess that Jesus is King of their lives. Jesus "always [did] the things that [were] pleasing to [the Father]" (John 8:29). Christians likewise "observe all that [Jesus] commanded" (Matt. 28:20).

When to Become a Christian

The Bible does not give a specific age. Scripture shows children to be innocent (Ezek. 18:20; Matt. 19:14). Babies, toddlers, and children do things that are wrong. They lie, they steal, and they hit. Children may know what a lie is or that toys are to be shared. They may know that hitting is a "no no." But children are not sinners. Adults are. Adults are accountable for their deeds (2 Cor. 5:10).

Somewhere in the middle we make this transition. We "know enough to refuse evil and choose good" (Isa. 7:16).

So what is the difference? Choosing. Choosing good or choosing evil. Eve is a good example. She demonstrates a comprehension of God's will, and the consequences of her choice. Satan asks her, "Has God said, 'You shall not eat from any tree of the garden?'" (Gen. 3:1). Eve responds, "From the fruit of the trees of the garden we may eat; but from the fruit of the tree which is in the middle of the garden, God has said, 'You shall not eat from it or touch it, lest you die'" (Gen. 3:2-3). Eve is not only able to give a memorized response, a catechistic answer, but she can also explain God's commandment in her own words.

Maybe you know the plan of salvation. Maybe you know a person must hear the gospel, believe it, repent of their sins, confess his faith, and be baptized. Maybe you have heard these five steps repeated so often you have them memorized. But do you know what they mean? Can you explain these commandments in your own words? When you think you are ready, and maybe you are, speak to an older Christian about your understanding of these commands.[1]

Conclusion

What trapeze artist, once he lets go of the bar, would refuse the safety of his partner's catch? Though he is flipping, flying, and in the moment having fun, to refuse his partner is foolish. So is life. We can live it to its fullest only when Jesus is living in us.

Questions
Short Answer

1. List some blessings that only Christians have. _____
_____
_____

2. How did Adam and Eve die the day they ate of the forbidden fruit?_____
_____

3. What do Christians have to hope in? _____

4. How does God guide Christians? _____

5. What must a person do to be saved?_____
_____

6. Where did God put every spiritual blessing? _____
_____

7. What does the Bible say people are baptized into? _____

8. How is our confession similar to the good confession Jesus made? _____
_____

---

[1] Mark Roberts has written a short study booklet on this subject entitled, *Am I ready?*, Lower Lights Publications.

9. Why are little children innocent even when they do bad things? _____
_____

10. How did Eve demonstrate she knew the meaning of God's command? ____
_____

True of False

_____ 1. Being free in Christ means being free to do whatever we want.

_____ 2. Repentance and baptism are both necessary in order to be saved.

_____ 3. The age of accountability is always twelve.

_____ 4. The only time we need to confess Jesus is before we are baptized.

_____ 5. I can faithfully follow Jesus without faithfully attending worship services.

Thought Question

Read the verses that follow and discuss what they teach about repentance (Joel
2:12-13; Jonah 3:5-8; Matt. 21:28-32)._____
_____
_____

The Main Attraction
How to Treat People

It's what people come to see, the main attraction, Jumbo the giant elephant. Maybe it's not the elephants, but whatever the main attraction is it makes the circus great.

How we treat people is our own main attraction. It is what we are known by. Are we kind or cruel? Are we humble or arrogant? Are we selfless or do we seek our own? In this lesson therefore, we will discuss treating people with kindness, humility, and selflessness. We will discuss treating others with love, no matter who they are, and no matter how they treat us.

The Greatest Commandment

Jesus was asked once about the greatest commandment. What was the main attraction in God's law? Jesus answered, "You shall love the Lord your God with all your heart, and with all your soul, and with all your mind" (Matt. 22:37). Then Jesus added the second. "You shall love your neighbor as yourself" (Matt. 22:39).

All of God's commandments are important. It is important to obey our parents when we are young, and honor them when we are old (Eph. 6:1-2; 1 Tim. 5:3-4). It is important to obey the laws of the land (Rom. 13:1; Matt. 22:21); to be generous with the poor (Matt. 5:42); to worship the Lord and him only (Matt. 4:10). But these, and every other commandment, are secondary, not less important, but the natural outcome of the two Jesus gave. If you love God, and your neighbor, you will worship, be generous, and obey.

Love is the source of action. If I love you I will be patient and kind to you. If I don't, I won't. The Bible says, "God is love" (1 John 4:8). It is because of this love that God gave His only begotten Son (John 3:16). It is because of this love that God then told us about Jesus, His sacrifice, and salvation (Heb. 1:2). It is because of this love that God now calls us to repentance and to Himself (Acts 17:30; 2 Pet. 3:9).

Even God's discipline comes from love. The Hebrew writer said, "My son, do not regard lightly the discipline of the Lord, nor faint when you are reproved by Him; for those whom the Lord loves He disciplines, and He scourges every son whom He receives" (Prov. 3:11-12; Heb. 12:5-6). We know that God disciplines us out of love from the fact that our own fathers disciplined us (Heb. 12:9). A good father disciplines his son not because the father enjoys discipline, but because the son needs discipline and the father wants what is best for his son (Prov. 13:24; Matt. 7:9-11).

Of Love and Like

How we treat people starts with how we love them. But to many, love is just a greater form of like. First you like someone. Then you really like them. Finally, if you like them long enough, you love them. But this is not God's love. This is not Bible love. Of course, you can speak of love in this way. I like ice cream, but I love strawberry swirl. But this is not the way Jesus uses the term love when He says, "Love your neighbor as yourself." Neither is this what John has in mind when he says, "God is love." In fact,

> **Love is not a feeling we fall into or out of. Love is intentionally doing what is right.**

God may not even like some of us. Think about that for awhile. At times God may not like any of us. There are people and things God hates (Psa. 5:5; Isa. 1:14; 61:8; Mal. 2:16). Still God loves us. Each of us. All of us. Because God does what is right for us.

It is in this framework, of doing what is right for others, that the apostle Paul writes, "Love is patient, love is kind, and is not jealous; love does not brag and is not arrogant, does not act unbecomingly; it does not seek its own, is not provoked, does not take into account a wrong suffered, does not rejoice in unrighteousness, but rejoices with the truth; bears all things, believes all things, hopes all things, endures all things" (1 Cor. 13:4-7).

None of these characteristics is an emotion. None are *like* statements. Love is not a feeling we fall into or out of. Love is intentionally doing what is right. If I love God I will keep His commandments (John 14:15). Paul says, "He who loves his neighbor has fulfilled the law. For this, 'You shall not commit adultery, you shall not murder, you shall not steal, you shall not covet' and if there is any other commandment, it is summed up in this saying, 'You shall love your neighbor as yourself'"(Rom. 13:8-9). I do not want my neighbor to commit adultery against me. I do not want him to violate, flirt with, or fantasize about my wife, so I will do what is right toward him. I will not violate, flirt with, or fantasize about his wife. I do not want my neighbor to murder me, so I will be peaceable with him. I do not want my neighbor to steal from me, so I will respect what is his.

Specific Neighbors

Now let's get to the heavy lifting. Let's apply this love, this doing what is right for our neighbor, toward some specific neighbors.

Married couples are neighbors. They are to love one another (Eph. 5:25; Titus 2:4). Love in a marriage will involve many things, but consider the application Peter makes for husbands. "Live with your wives in an understanding way, as with a weaker vessel" (1 Pet. 3:7). Peter is not commenting on a woman's physic. He is illustrating his point. Husbands ought to be gentle with their wives just as they would handle a special and fragile dish with extra care. A man ought to speak to his wife with kindness, even if she can handle nastiness from other people. A man ought to carry the groceries in and the trash out, even if his wife is strong enough to do it herself. A man ought to put the seat down, even if his wife is smart enough to look first.

Christians are neighbors too, and as neighbors they love one another. This phrase "Love one another" is found twelve times in the New Testament. Peter modifies it once and writes, "love the brotherhood" (1 Pet. 2:17). Christians pray for the sick (James 5:14-15). They visit the orphans and widows, as if Jesus were one of them (Matt. 25:34-40; James 1:27). They encourage the week and restore the fallen (Gal. 6:1). Christians serve one another.

This love is not dependant on our neighbor's race, affluence, or influence. Paul says, "There is no distinction between Jew and Greek; for the same Lord is Lord of all" (Rom. 10:12). Again he says, "Instruct those who are rich in this present world not to be conceited or to fix their hope on the uncertainty of riches, but on God, who richly supplies us with all things to enjoy. Instruct them to do good, to be rich in good works, to be generous and ready to share" (1 Tim. 6:17-18). Jesus says, "whoever wishes to be first among you shall be slave of all" (Mark 10:44).

Finally, Jesus says, "Love your enemies, do good to those who hate you, bless those who curse you, pray for those who mistreat you" (Luke 6:27-28). If I cannot love my wife as my first neighbor or my brother as my friend, then I will love them as my enemy. I will do what is right to them, even if they mistreat me.

If a man's wife does not behave like a wife should he is not excused from his responsibility. If a Christian's brother is self-willed and quick-tempered the Christian is not permitted to respond in kind. Peter says, "To sum up, let all be harmonious, sympathetic, brotherly, kindhearted, and humble in spirit; not returning evil for evil, or insult for insult, but giving a blessing instead" (1 Pet. 3:8-9). Their sins do not justify ours. We are to love our neighbor as our self, whether that neighbor is our wife, a fellow Christian, or an enemy.

Conclusion

The circus is not much without its main attraction, and neither are we. We may make an impressive show with our intelligence, charm, or physique. But if we do not love God and our fellow man the show is bankrupt.

Questions

Short Answer

1. Why does Jesus say love is the greatest commandment? _____
_____

2. What did love cause God to do? _____
_____

3. How can discipline, specifically punishments, be considered acts of love?___
_____

4. When people say they love ice cream what do they mean?_____
_____

5. List the characteristics Paul attributes to love. _____
_____
_____

6. How does love prevent a man from committing adultery, theft, and murder?
_____
_____

7. Why does Peter compare a man's wife to a weaker vessel?_____
_____

8. What do Christians do for one another that shows love? _____
_____

9. What makes a Christian great (Mark 10:44)?_____
_____

10. Is there any one we do not need to love? _____
_____

True False

_____ 1. Love is a greater form of like.
_____ 2. We can only serve Christians if they are of the same race as we are.
_____ 3. The greatest people have the most servants.
_____ 4. If you love your enemies they will become your friends.

_____ 5. We can be good to people even if they are not good to us.

Thought Question

What do you think makes some people our enemies? _____
_____

_____

A Painted on Smile
Friendship

Some like the clowns. Some like their rubber noses, and oversized shoes. Some like their painted on smiles, and the gags they play on one another. But be careful of choosing friends like clowns, friends who seem fun, but who are only wearing a painted on smile.

In this lesson we will talk about friendship. We will look at some friendships in the Bible. We will then discuss some aspects of being a friend, and choosing good friends.

Bible Friends

Making a simple bibliography of some of the friendships found in the Bible can show us a lot about how to be a friend and how to choose friends wisely. One of the most famous friendships is that of David and Jonathan. Jonathan was the son of king Saul, and heir to the Israelite throne. God however, chose David to be the next king. This might have caused a rift or power struggle to arise between other friends, but not between David and Jonathan. When Jonathan was killed in battle his friend David said, "I am distressed for you, my brother Jonathan; you have been very pleasant to me. Your love to me was more wonderful than the love of women" (2 Sam. 1:26).

> Jehoshaphat's poor choice in friends hurt more people than himself.

Paul and Barnabas are another pair of friends. Barnabas vouched for Paul when no Christian in Jerusalem wanted anything to do with him (Acts 9:26-27). They traveled together, taught together, and were persecuted together (Acts 11:26). But their friendship cooled over a difference of opinion (Acts 15:36-40).

Ahab and Jehoshaphat were friends too, but these friends should have separated. Ahab was a wicked king of Israel. Jehoshaphat was a righteous king of Judah. These friends had their children marry each other. Jehoshaphat's son Jehoram married Athaliah, Ahab's daughter. When Jehoram latter became king the Bible says, "he walked in the ways of the kings of Israel, just as the house of Ahab had done" (2 Kings 8:18). Jehoshaphat's poor choice in friends hurt more people than himself.

On Being Friendly

"A man that hath friends must shew himself friendly" (Prov. 18:24 KJV)[1]. This is an obvious truism, and there are many examples that illustrate it. For instance, people flocked to Jesus early on because He was nice. He healed the sick, fed the hungry, noticed the outcast, and picked up those who stumbled (John 6:2, 5-12, 4:7, 8:4-11). This does not negate that fact that Jesus criticized the scribes and Pharisees for their hypocrisy (Matt. 23:13-33), or that He rebuked the crowds for following Him just for bread (John 6:26-27). But Jesus was friendly, and like Jesus, friendly people will make friends.

There are three aspects of being friendly that I specifically want to address. First of all, friendly people are happy. Happiness, along with its tell-tale smile, draws people. Debi Pearl, in a book she has written for women, tells about an ugly woman that drew crowds of admiring men. The woman worked in a hardware store and was, as Pearl describes her, more than just regular ugly, she was "hillbilly ugly."[2] But she was also happy, and it was this cheerful disposition that made her so attractive. When Paul wrote to fellow Christians he exhibited this same friendly attitude. Even while he was in prison Paul said, "Rejoice in the Lord always; and again I will say, rejoice" (Phil. 4:4).

Friendly people are also interested in others. When Jesus passed through Samaria He sat down at a well. A Samaritan woman came to the same well to draw water. When she did Jesus didn't ignore her. He spoke to her. He asked her for a drink of water (John 4:7). Eventually Jesus was able to teach her the truth. This story is a good lesson in personal evangelism, and personal evangelism begins with being interested in other people, interested in their souls. It begins with being friendly.

---

[1] While the statement, "A man that hath friends must shew himself friendly" is a true principle, it is more accurately translated, "A man of many friends comes to ruin." The verse is contrasting the man of many worthless friends with the man with a single true friend.

[2] Debi Pearl, *Help Meet,* 27.

Most of all, friendly people are genuine. They are genuinely happy. They genuinely care about other people. They are not like the Cheshire Cat. It was always smiling at Alice. It was so interested in Alice. But it was notorious for getting Alice into trouble. The Cheshire Cat was not friendly. Absalom, the son of king David, flattered people, but he was not friendly. He was a fake. He was a *good mixer*.[3] He won people over, and "stole away the hearts of the men of Israel" (2 Sam. 15:6) with charm. But he did not care for the people. His interests were selfish.

Real friends, genuine friends, sometimes have to hurt one another's feelings in order to help each other do what is right (2 Sam. 12:7; Mark 8:33; Gal. 2:11; 4:16). The Bible says, "Faithful are the wounds of a friend, but deceitful are the kisses of an enemy" (Prov. 27:6).

The Influence of Friends

Friendly people will make friends, but these newfound friends will also influence them. Who we become close to, become buddies with, will impact who we are. It is important therefore, for us to choose friends who will build us up and encourage us towards godliness.

Jesus influenced His disciples for good. The Bible says, "Now as [the Council] observed the confidence of Peter and John, and understood that they were uneducated and untrained men, they were marveling, and began to recognize them as having been with Jesus" (Acts 4:13). The confidence of Peter and John made the Council think of Jesus. Jesus had impressed His image, or character on Peter and John.

Christians likewise are to be, "conformed to the image of [Jesus]" (Rom. 8:29). Just as Peter and John spent time with Jesus, watching and listening to Him, Christians do too. Christians listen to Jesus, by listening to the word of God (Heb. 1:2). They mature and become more like Jesus by obeying it (2 Tim. 2:15; James 1:22-25; 1 Pet. 2:2; 2 Pet. 3:18).

Christians also spend time with one another. They make friends with one another. Just as Peter and John spent time with Jesus in the flesh, Christians spend time with Jesus' body, the church. Christians meet together to worship and encourage one another (Heb. 10:24-25; 1 Thess. 5:11). Christians eat together (Acts 2:46). Christians work together (Acts 18:3). Christians weep and rejoice together (Rom. 12:15), and someday Christians will go to heaven together (1 Thess. 4:13-18).

Christians however, need to be careful of friendship with the world (James 4:4). Paul warns, "Do not be deceived: 'Bad company corrupts good morals'" (1 Cor. 15:33). We cannot play in the water and not become wet. We cannot bathe

---

[3] R. L. Whiteside (1955). *A Good Mixer, Doctrinal Discourses*, 35.

in the sun and not become hot. And we cannot wallow in the world and not become worldly. We deceive ourselves when we think otherwise.

Who we choose to spend time with will influence who we are. It is true that we are to influence those around us for good. Jesus calls His people the "salt of the earth" and the "light of the world" (Matt. 5:13, 14). We cannot influence the world by isolating ourselves from it (John 17:15). But we do not need to be buddies with the world. We do not need to act like the world, dress like the world, or dream the dreams of the world. We do not need to chase the approval of the world. Because if we do the "salt [will have] become tasteless...[and] good for nothing anymore, except to be thrown out and trampled under foot by men" (Matt. 5:13).

The wisdom of the Psalms begins with these words. "How blessed is the man who does not walk in the counsel of the wicked, nor stand in the path of sinners, nor sit in the seat of scoffers" (Ps. 1:1). This is faithful advice still today.

Conclusion

Friends are an important part of life. Making friends with people who will build us up and whom we can encourage will make life fun. But be careful of those who only wear a painted on smile.

Questions
Short Answer

1. How did God's choice to make David king instead of Jonathan affect David and Jonathan's friendship? _____

_____

2. How did Barnabas treat Paul when he first came to Jerusalem? _____

_____

3. How did Jehoshaphat's friendship with Ahab affect Jehoshaphat's family? __

_____

4. Where was Paul when he said Christians should rejoice?_____

_____

5. What is a good mixer?_____

_____

6. Why are the wounds of a friend better than the kisses of an enemy? _____

_____

7. What did spending time with Jesus do for Peter and John? _____

_____

8. Why does Paul warn us not to be deceived? _____

_____

9. How can becoming like the world ruin our influence on the world? _____

_____

10. Who does the psalmist say the blessed man is?_____
_____

True or False

_____ 1. Paul and Barnabas remained friends even though they had a disagree-
ment.

_____ 2. Jesus spoke to the woman at the well first.

_____ 3. Being friendly means we will never hurt people's feelings.

_____ 4. Jesus influenced the lives of Peter and John.

_____ 5. We can act like the world and not be worldly.

Thought Question

How can having friends who are Christians help us to be godly? _____
_____
_____
_____

The Strongman
Anger

That dumbbell is not filled with air. The strongman's muscles are not either. The strongman is strong. More than controlling hundreds of pounds though, the true strongman exercises control over another weight. The real strongman controls his anger.

In this lesson we will see how anger compounds itself with other sins. I will offer some suggestions about how to control anger. I will also suggest that there is a time and way for us to be angry.

When Anger is King

King Saul was a commanding man. He was the giant of Israel. He stood head and shoulders above everyone else (1 Sam. 9:2). He was Israel's king, and when he called, God's people came "as one man" (1 Sam. 11:7). Saul however, for all of his strength and influence, was not in control. Anger was. Saul was an angry man. Twice he nearly pinned his son-in-law David to the wall with a spear (1 Sam. 18:11). In a rage he tried to kill his own son (1 Sam. 20:33).

> Many men, like Saul, are angry men. Anger rules their lives because they will not rule their anger.

Saul is not unique. His choice of outlet might be, but his anger problem is not. Many men, like Saul, are angry men. Anger rules their lives because they will not rule their anger.

The problem with anger is compounded because anger does not rule alone. When Israel demanded a king God allowed it. God also commanded Samuel to tell the people what a king would bring. He would bring the appearance of national success, but more. A king would bring loss, misery, and taxes. A king would take more than the people expected, or were willing to give (1 Sam. 8:5-18). When anger is allowed to rule it "give[s] the devil an opportunity" (Eph. 4:27).

Paul lists a number of sins in his letter to the Galatians. He writes, "Now the deeds of the flesh are evident, which are . . . enmities, strife, jealousy, outbursts of anger, disputes, dissensions, factions, envying . . . and things like these" (Gal.

5:19-21). Anger is in the middle of these sins. It feeds them and feeds off of them. This is why Jesus said, "everyone who is angry with his brother shall be guilty" (Matt. 5:22). This is true of John as well. He wrote, "Everyone who hates his brother is a murderer" (1 John 3:15). Anger leads to hate. Hate leads to murder. Lastly, murder leads to death.

Cain was angry and murdered his brother Abel (Gen. 4:5-8). Joseph's brothers were jealous and would have murdered him, if the opportunity to sell him had not arisen (Gen. 37:3, 4, 11, 18-28). King Ahab envied his neighbor's vineyard. His neighbor was soon falsely accused and stoned to death (1 Kings 21:1-16). Daniel was thrown into the den of lions (Dan. 6). John the Baptist was beheaded (Mark 6:14-28). Jesus was crucified (Mark 15:10). Paul was chased from city to city (Acts 9:23-30, 13:45-50, 14:4-6, 19, 17:5-14). All of this happened because anger and its accompanying sins ruled the lives of some.

Taking Control

Anger does not have to rule our lives. Like every temptation and sin, anger can be controlled. Paul wrote, "No temptation has overtaken you but such as is common to man; and God is faithful, who will not allow you to be tempted beyond what you are able" (1 Cor. 10:13).

Anger is a common problem. King Saul is still not unique. Jesus was "tempted in all things as we are" (Heb. 4:15). The specific situations differ, but when people misrepresented Jesus, used Him, and made fun of Him wasn't Jesus tempted? Of course, but Jesus did not let anger rule His life.

We have no control over how others behave. We cannot make them do what is right, but we can control how we respond. Paul wrote, "I buffet my body and make it my slave" (1 Cor. 9:27). Solomon said, "Like a city that is broken into and without walls is a man who has no control over his spirit" (Prov. 25:28).

We control ourselves by giving control away. Not to anger, but giving control to God (Col. 3:15). Jesus did (John 8:29; Matt. 26:39). Paul did. He said his "ambition, whether at home or absent, [was] to be pleasing to [the Lord]" (2 Cor. 5:9). Solomon too came to the same conclusion (Eccl. 12:13).

Prayer is a major part of a godly person's life (Dan. 6:10; Acts 10:2; 1 Thess. 5:17). Giving God control of our lives means we will begin praying a lot about a lot of things. One specific thing we will pray for is the wellbeing of those who persecute us (Matt. 5:44). While Jesus was on the cross, being insulted, He prayed, "Father, forgive them; for they do not know what they are doing" (Luke 23:34). Jesus did not let anger rule His life. Jesus did what was pleasing to the Father. When Stephen was stoned he followed the example of Jesus and prayed, "Lord, do not hold this sin against them" (Acts 7:60).

It is impossible to hate people and love them at the same time. It is hard to curse people and want to punch, choke, and kick them while asking God bless them. Only one attitude will win out, and much will depend on which we give the most time to.

There Is a Time For Anger

Controlling our anger is hard. It is a stumbling block that many have in common. But another problem many have with anger is failing to be angry when they should be.

Paul wrote, "Be angry, and yet do not sin" (Eph. 4:26). Anger is a problem when it is mishandled. We retaliate with meanness. That is an unrighteous anger that "does not achieve the righteousness of God" (James 1:20). But there is a righteous anger.

Paul spoke about peace, forbearance, longsuffering, joy, love, and every other sweet behavior, but he also was angry when it was right to be angry. When Peter came to Antioch Paul, "opposed him to his face" (Gal. 2:11). Had Peter barrowed Paul's tunic without asking? Had he cut in line at the food court, or bumped into Paul knocking all the scrolls out of Paul's arm? No. Paul confronted Peter, "because [Peter] stood condemned. For prior to the coming of certain men from James, he used to eat with the Gentiles; but when they came, he began to withdraw and hold himself aloof . . . [and] they were not straightforward about the truth of the gospel" (Gal. 2:11-14). Paul was not angry because Paul was wronged. Paul was angry because Peter hurt the truth, the gospel, and God.

Jesus endured personal insults, and stayed on the cross[1]. Jesus however, did not tolerate God being insulted, or His house being misused (John 2:13-17). David spared the life of Saul, his personal enemy (1 Sam. 24:4, 26:12). He was gracious to Mephibosheth, a royal rival (2 Sam. 9:6-13), but David also prayed for the death of other enemies (Ps. 139:19-22). It seems odd that David would do this. Think about it though. Why were those he wanted dead his enemies? They were not his enemies because of a personal grudge. They were his enemies because they were first God's enemies. Even Saul "became very angry" (1 Sam. 11:6) because God's people were being attacked.

Christians have no business fighting or brawling. Not when they themselves are insulted or when the Lord is attacked. God has said, "Vengeance is Mine, I will repay" (Rom. 12:19). But it is right to be angry with those who take God's

---

[1] Aside from the fact that His once loyal disciple abandoned Him (Matt. 26:33, 35, 56), and the people chose a murderer rather than the life giving spirit (Matt. 27:17-22) here are some passages containing the insults leveled against Jesus: Mathew 26:61, 67, 68; 27:27-31, 39-44.

name in vain, who dismember Christ's body with factions, and "who trample under foot the Son of God" (Heb. 10:29). It is right to be angry. It is right to speak out against them. It is right to oppose them.

Conclusion

The strongman is strong, but it takes a stronger man to control his anger. It takes a real strongman to pray for his enemies, to overlook personal insults, and when it is time to be angry to know it and to act.

Questions

Short Answer

1. How is anger mishandled? _____
_____

2. What did Saul do when he was angry? _____
_____

3. What does anger give the devil an opportunity to do? _____
_____

4. How is everyone who hates his brother a murderer? _____
_____

5. How was Jesus tempted in all things like we are? _____
_____

6. To what is a man compared who has no control over his spirit? _____
_____

7. What will praying for our enemies do for us? _____
_____

8. Why was Paul angry with Peter? _____
_____

9. Why did David pray for the death of his enemies? _____
_____

10. What should make Christians angry, and what should they do about it?____
_____

True or False

_____ 1. Anger works with other sins like jealously and envy.

_____ 2. Uncontrolled anger has often led to murder.

_____ 3. Praying for our enemies makes it harder to hate them.

_____ 4. Jesus was never angry.

_____ 5. Christians should punch people who take God's name in vain.

Thought Question

Why do you think Jesus and Stephen both prayed for their enemies just before they died? _____

The Fire-Eater
The Tongue

How does he not burn himself? How does he keep the fire from singeing his eyebrows? That must be why I have never seen a fire-eater with a beard and mustache. Well, however much facial hair he has left the fire-eater must be careful. When James compares the tongue with a fire he is making the same point. The tongue can burn a lot of people besides the man in whose mouth it is. So James says, "let everyone be quick to hear, slow to speak" (James 1:19). That is, be careful.

In this lesson we will see the great power the tongue has. We will see how some words help, and others hurt. Then I will give some specific *dos* and *don'ts* of speaking.

A Powerful Tool

The Bible is a book of speeches. Deuteronomy is a series of sermons Moses preaches before he dies. The prophetical books are sermons too. The gospels narrate Jesus' life, but they also record Jesus' famous Sermon on the Mount, His parables, His prayer, His rant against the Pharisees, and His will for the disciples (Matt. 5-7; 13:3-23; John 17; Matt. 23; 28:18-20). The history of the church is told in the book of Acts, as Luke moves from speech to speech. The church begins with Peter's sermon on Pentecost (Acts 2:14-40). A great persecution comes against the church after Stephen's speech and martyrdom (Acts 7:2-53). The disciples learn the will of God concerning circumcision, and the Law of Moses in the Jerusalem debate (Acts 15:7-21). The gospel even spreads to the remotest parts of the world through Paul's sermons in Athens, to the Ephesian elders, and those before Felix, Festus, and King Agrippa II (Acts 17:22-31; 20:18-35; 24:25; 26:2-29).

These speeches motivate us to greater faithfulness, like good preaching should. Joshua said, "Choose for yourselves today whom you will serve . . . but as for me and my house, we will serve the Lord" (Josh. 24:15). I want to serve with Joshua. The valley of dead, dried out bones were raised up to new

life because God's word was preached to them (Ezek. 37). I want to preach the life giving gospel message. Peter and John "began to speak the word of God with boldness" (Acts 4:31) even though they had been threatened by the same people who killed Jesus. I want to do the same though atheists, and biblical liberals mock.

Words can also hurt. They can keep us from action, and weaken our faith. Ten spies demoralized the whole congregation of Israel and kept them from entering the Promised Land (Num. 13:31). Delilah wore Samson down with her constant nagging so that he finally told her the secret of his great strength (Judg. 16:16-17). Jezebel rattled Elijah so much with one statement that the tough old prophet crawled in a cave and hid. He had rebuked King Ahab for troubling Israel (1 Kings 18:18). He had faced four hundred fifty false prophets on Mount Carmel (1 Kings 18:19-40), yet Jezebel's words scared him (1 Kings 19:2-9).

Some Dos and Don'ts
James wrote, "the tongue is a small part of the body, and yet it boasts of great things. Behold, how great a forest is set aflame by such a small fire! And the tongue is a fire" (James 3:5-6). Since the power of our words is so great we must choose them with care. Following are some dos and don'ts of word choosing.

Half-Truths
God does not distinguish big lies from little ones, or lies that harm from those that protect. God does not separate the occasional liars from the lying addicts. God has said, "But for . . . all liars, their part will be in the lake that burns with fire and brimstone" (Rev. 21:8).

What about half-truths though? Are they really lies, they are half true? Every half-truth is also half lie, and the lie is the more significant half. When Abraham met Abimelech, "Abraham said of Sarah his wife, 'She is my sister.' So Abimelech king of Gerar sent and took Sarah" (Gen. 20:2). Abraham later explained, "she actually is my sister, the daughter of my father, but not the daughter of my mother" (Gen. 20:13). While Sarah was Abraham's sister, the fact that she was Abraham's wife was the more important relationship to both Abraham and Abimelech.

Vulgarity
Jokes do not need to be sexual to be funny. Expletives do not need to be added to every statement. Paul wrote, "there must be no filthiness and silly talk, or coarse jesting" (Eph. 5:4). Keeping our speech free of vulgarity can be hard because so many people are filthy and coarse. Their language can become ours without us realizing it. This is why the movies we watch, the music we listen to, and the people we associate with are so important. Jesus said, "the mouth speaks out of that which fills the heart" (Matt. 12:34).

Euphemisms

God is holy so He and His name must be treated with special reverence (Lev. 11:44-45; 1 Pet. 1:16). God Himself said, "You shall not take the name of the Lord your God in vain" (Exod. 20:7). This is not to prohibit the use of God's name, but the casual use of it. This was to keep the Hebrews from making God's name common, an ordinary punctuation of joy or anger as it has become today.

Euphemisms are special ways people make God's name common. They are more socially acceptable terms, but not acceptable to God. Instead of saying God's name a person might replace it with, *gosh*, *gee*, or *golly*. This might be more acceptable to some, saying *gosh* in place of God, but it is still saying the same thing. Slapping God across the face is insulting, but shaking the back of our hand at Him says the same thing.

Confessing Jesus

Confessing our faith is part of the plan of salvation. Paul wrote, "With the mouth confession is made" (Rom. 10:10). Jesus said, "Everyone therefore who shall confess Me before men, I will also confess him before My Father who is in heaven" (Matt. 10:32). The Ethiopian eunuch's confession is a good example of this (Acts 8:37).

Confessing Jesus however, goes beyond the moment before we are baptized. Three specific times Peter was given the chance to confess Jesus. Peter was not about to be baptized. He was not standing before a group of Christians and friends. No, but Peter had an opportunity to confess Jesus, and he chose to deny Him instead (John 18:15-17; 25-27).

Edifying

Words that edify are words that encourage and build other people up. Paul said, "Let no unwholesome word proceed from your mouth, but only such a word as is good for edification" (Eph. 4:29).

Being respectful is a good way to edify others. Again Paul said, "Do not sharply rebuke an older man, but rather appeal to him as a father" (1 Tim. 5:1-2). Speaking in Bible class and adding to the discussion encourages the teacher and builds up the class. Singing loud and adding our Amen to the prayer edifies the church (Eph. 5:19; 1 Cor. 14:16).

Please and Thank You

When we pray and ask God to "give us this day our daily bread, [to] forgive us our debts...[and to] deliver us from evil" we show our dependence on God for these things (Matt. 6:11-3). When we pray and "in everything give thanks" we acknowledge that what we have comes from God (1 Thess. 5:18; James 1:17). A healthy prayer life keeps these facts in our minds. Saying *please* and *thank you* does the same, since none of us lives completely independent of others.

Conclusion

I do not know how the fire-eater does not burn himself. I do not know if he has some trick. Maybe it is only by training and care. What I do know is that constant care with our words is the only way to keep from burning someone with them.

Questions
Short Answer

1. What did Joshua say he would do?_____

2. How were the dry bones in Ezekiel's vision resurrected? _____

3. What did Jezebel say to Elijah that caused him to hide in a cave?_____

4. To what does James compare the tongue? _____

5. What did Abimelech want to know about Abraham and Sarah's relationship?

6. How do movies and music influence our language? _____

7. What does it mean to take God's name in vain? _____

8. Where was Peter when he denied Jesus?_____

9. What does edify mean?_____

10. How does saying *please* and *thank you* show our dependence on other people?_____

True or False

_____ 1. James says we are to be quick to speak.
_____ 2. A half-truth is also a half lie.
_____ 3. It is better to say *gosh* than *God*.
_____ 4. We must only confess Jesus once.
_____ 5. Only adults can edify the church.

Thought Question

Read James 3:7-8. Why can the tongue never be tamed? _____
_____
_____
_____

Behind the Elephants
Work and Money

Every man needs a respectable job. Maybe it is blue collar. Maybe it is white. Maybe it is in a factory. Maybe it is flipping burgers. Maybe it is sweeping up behind the elephants at the circus. Whatever it is, any work a man can do that is honest and provides for his own, is respectable work.

In this lesson we will see why every man needs a job. We will address some points a man should think about when looking for a job. We will also talk about handling the money we earn by working a job.

Why Work

Work is a bad word, a four-letter word, to some people. But work is not bad. It may be dirty, but it is not bad. Neither is work God's punishment for sin. The difficulty did increase (Gen. 3:17-19), but Adam was to "cultivate and keep" the garden even before he sinned (Gen. 2:15).

God gave Adam a job because every man needs to work. Every man needs to be productive. We need to have something to do. There are several reason for this.

First, working is God's way of providing the necessities of life: food, clothing, and shelter. God told Adam he would have to work before he could eat (Gen. 3:19). Paul made the same point saying, "If anyone will not work, neither let him eat" (2 Thess. 3:10). "If anyone does not provide for his own, and especially for those of his household, he has denied the faith" (1 Tim. 5:8).

Working enables us to share. Paul said, "Let him who steals steal no longer; but rather let him labor, performing with his own hands what is good, in order that he may have something to share with him who has need" (Eph. 4:28). Someone may ask, "How can anyone have need if everyone works?" The answer is that, some *cannot* work and are therefore in need, but these are different than those who *will* not work.

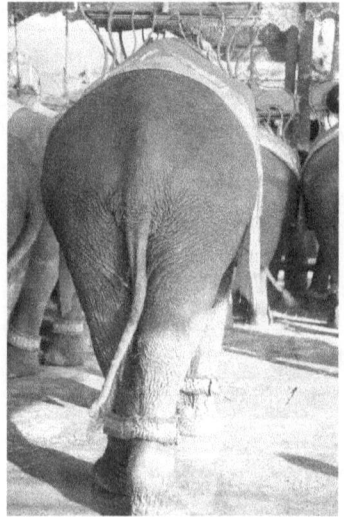

Working enables us to support the gospel financially. On the first day of the week the disciples gave money to provide for needy Christians (1 Cor. 16:1-2). Caring for these is part of the local church's work. Preaching the gospel is too. The church at Philippi gave money to Paul (Phil. 4:15). Paul also said to Timothy, "Those who work hard at preaching and teaching [are] worthy of [their] wages" (1 Tim. 5:17-18). This money does not come from a bake sale, a car wash, or selling "Juleps for Jesus" at the Kentucky Derby. The local church raises this money the way God provided, the weekly freewill offering of Christians.

We also find identity in our work. One of the few things we know about Cain and Abel is their occupation. "Abel was a keeper of flocks but Cain was a tiller of the ground" (Gen. 4:2). Jesus was not just the son of a carpenter, but was a carpenter Himself (Matt. 13:55; Mark 6:3). Even a man that will not work is identified by his lack of work. He is bum, a deadbeat, or, as he is called in the Bible, a sluggard (Prov. 26:13).

Choosing A Job

If you can be paid for doing what you like that is always best. But what intrigues us may not provide a living. In this case there are some other work related factors to consider.

First, whatever job you take, the work must be moral. Prostitution and theft were ways of making a living in Bible times. They are the same today, but neither is moral. Christians have no business in this work or work like it. For instance, pornography is to prostitution what gambling is to theft. Gambling is taking from someone else what he does not want to give up. It is stealing by consent. If theft is wrong and gambling is wrong, what about working in the gaming industry? Here is a similar question. Since drunkenness is wrong, is working for a brewery sinful too?

Work should not keep us from worship. God commands us to meet with the church and worship together (Heb. 10:25). When God commanded Israel to observe the Passover He also provided an alternate time for those who could not for extenuating circumstances (Num. 9:6-13).[1] There may be occasions when we cannot meet with the church. We are ill. The car breaks down, or we stop to help someone else who is having car trouble. We may have to work late on occasion, but if our job continues to keep us from the Lord, should we look for another job?

Whatever job you find then, remember, "do your work heartily, as for the Lord rather than for men" (Col. 3:23). It is not about what others see, what the

---

[1] What the unclean men do not ask is the interesting part of their question. They do not ask as some church members would, "Do I have to attend every service" but "why are we restrained from presenting the offering of the Lord as its appointed time?" They wanted to worship.

boss sees, or what you can get by without doing. Work, like every other part of life, is about pleasing the Lord.

Money, Materialism, and the Measure of Success

Money is not the root of evil. The love of money is (1 Tim. 6:10), because love is blind, love deceives. Money promises happiness, but can only buy pleasure. It promises friends, but can only afford company. It promises safety, but can only secure locks. Using wealth to gauge success then is like letting the car salesmen decide what a good deal is.

Money and material things cannot measure success because life is not about money and material things. Jesus asked, "Is not life more than food, and the body than clothing?" (Matt. 6:25). The question was rhetorical and the obvious answer was yes. Life is about seeking God's kingdom (Matt. 6:33).

Success in this life is successfully providing for the next life. It is laying up treasure in heaven (Matt. 6:19-20). Lazarus was a poor beggar, but was he a failure (Luke 16:19-23)? Was Jesus? He was homeless (Luke 9:58). What about the apostle Paul? He gave up the worldly advantages he had "in view of the surpassing value of knowing Christ Jesus" (Phil. 3:8). This is the kind of question Jesus is asking when He said, "What will a man be profited, if he gains the whole world, and forfeits his soul? Or what will a man give in exchange for his soul?" (Matt. 16:26).

Of course there are also examples of righteous people who were rich. Abraham and Job are the best known. More often the examples are how riches destroy righteousness (Amos 4:1; Luke 12:15-21; James 5:4-6; Rev. 3:17). This is why wisdom says, "Give me neither poverty nor riches; feed me with the food that is my portion, lest I be full and deny Thee and say, 'Who is the Lord?' Or lest I be in want and steal, and profane the name of my God." (Prov. 30:8-9).

Saving and Spending

God has entrusted us with whatever we have, whether a little or a lot. He has put us in charge as stewards or managers of these material possessions. When we give an account of our deeds on the last day, we will have to account for how we have managed these possessions. I offer two suggestions.

First, remember it is all God's anyway so give to God's work generously (2 Cor. 9:6-7). In the Old Testament the Israelites were commanded to tithe or give ten percent (Lev. 27:30). In the New Testament God has not specified a percent, but percentage is implied in the words "as he may prosper" (1 Cor. 16:2). According to the increase of our blessings our giving should increase. What percent then does God want? A tenth is a good place to start, but we are blessed much more than the Israelites.

Second, we must learn to live within our means. Credit cards can be dangerous. They are easy to get, and easier to use. If we are not careful we can over spend and at twenty to thirty percent interest we can become the "slave of the lender" (Prov. 22:7, KJV).

Living within our means specifically means living with my means, not my parents' means, not my neighbors' means, but my means. When we start out on our own we do not have much. We do not have a house with a yard. We do not have furnishings for the house we do not have. Maybe we have an old car, but our parents have all of these things and more. Rather than being content with the little we can afford, or the used things we are given, we are tempted to buy a house like our parents' house, or better. We buy furnishings like theirs, but newer. Soon we lack only one thing, money for food.

Conclusion

Every man needs a job. He needs to provide for his own, and share with the needy. He needs to live in this world, but save for the next. If a man can do these things only by sweeping up behind the elephants, he has a respectable job.

Questions
Short Answer

1. What makes a job respectable? _____
_____

2. If a man will not work what else should he not do? _____
_____

3. What is wrong with working in a brewery? _____
_____

4. What do you think doing your work "heartily, as for the Lord" means? _____
_____

5. How is the love of money the root of all kinds of evil? _____
_____

6. What is a successful life? _____
_____

7. What worldly advantages did Paul give up for Christ? _____
_____

8. What is the danger of both poverty and riches? _____
_____

9. On what are we to base our giving to God? _____
_____

10. How can contentment help us live within our means? _____
_____

True or False

_____ 1. God punished Adam by making him work.

_____ 2. Work is more important than worship.

_____ 3. Life is all about food, clothing, and shelter.

_____ 4. It is hard for rich people to be righteous.

_____ 5. We are stewards or managers of our belongings.

Thought Question

Why is it more important to know Jesus than to have stuff? _____

_____

_____

_____

Taming the Beast
Sexuality

There is a rare group of men who, out of foolishness, fascination, or an addiction to adrenaline, wrestle all kinds of animals. The beasts often outweigh the men. They are more agile too. They have teeth, claws, and a crushing grip. But the men are able to tame the beasts.

Sexual temptation is a beast more vicious than any lion or bear. It is a dragon (Rev. 12:9). Satan is a cunning tempter (Gen. 3:1), and a hungry, restless lion (1 Pet. 5:8). Sexual temptation however, can be tamed. God told Cain, "sin is crouching at the door; and its desire is for you, but you must master it" (Gen. 4:7). Cain surrendered to temptation, but we do not have to. The apostle Paul wrote, "No temptation has overtaken you but such as is common to man; and God is faithful, who will not allow you to be tempted beyond what you are able, and with the temptation will provide the way of escape also, that you may be able to endure it" (1 Cor. 10:13).

In this chapter we will discuss some facts about sexual temptation and sin. I will then propose a simple, but sure way to tame these beasts.

The Abundance of Sexual Sin

Sexual temptation is everywhere. It is in the shopping malls. Retailers *undress* manikins in lingerie. They cover the windows with posters of uncovered women, dressed like harlots advertising a storewide sale (Prov. 7:10). Billboards feature forty horizontal feet of a Hooter's girl. The newspaper even brings two strippers home, in color and nearly nothing else, featured on the front cover above the fold.[1]

Even at home a man's eyes are not safe. The television show may be inno-

---

[1] May 4, 2006 *Lexington Herald Leader*, Disrobing for dollars

cent, but every few minutes a jeans commercial, car advertisement, or even soap will be promoted in a dirty way.[2] Then of course there is the Internet which is like a service station's toilet, useful when needed, but chances are when you open the door you will be staring at someone else's filth.

Silence, the Weapon of Sexual Sin

Sexual temptation and sin must be confronted. They must be dealt with. We must tame the beast, because it thrives in the dark and secret places only we ourselves know. The Bible says, "Men loved the darkness rather than the light; for their deeds were evil. For everyone who does evil hates the light, and does not come to the light, lest his deeds should be exposed" (John 3:19-20).

Therefore, expose them (Eph. 5:11). Call them by their names. Even Harry Potter understands this principle. The fear and power of the villain only grows while he is known as, "He who must not be named." But he must be named. To name sin is to strip it of its strength to hide, to fester, and to grow.

There are two beasts, two specific sins that we must name. The name of the first is pornography, and the name of the second is masturbation.

If we are struggling or caught by either no excuse will help. Solomon describes how the naïve youth, "pass[es] through the street near her corner; and he takes the way to her house, in the twilight, in the evening, in the middle of the night and in the darkness" (Prov. 7:8-9). Perhaps the man was unaware of who lived in that particular neighborhood. Maybe he did not know there were women who behaved so loosely. Maybe he was a good-hearted country boy on his first visit to the big city. Maybe he was just in the wrong place at the wrong time. Whatever innocent reason he was there, he lost his innocence when he stayed.

It does not matter if we went looking for pornography or stumbled across a box full.[3] It does not matter if an older boy showed us how to masturbate, or we discovered a reward for climbing the gym class rope. Whatever the reason we sin, it is in our hands to stop. We must admit our guilt before God and repent (1 John 1:9; Luke 13:3).

A Father's Responsibility

Fathers too have a huge responsibility in calling sin by its name. We must teach our sons. We must warn them about it.

Masturbation is difficult to talk about. It is difficult to write about. We expose our weaknesses. We may feel embarrassed about our own adolescence. If we are still masturbating we will feel hypocritical to teach our sons to resist. Still,

---

[2] Axe and other body washes for men.

[3] *The Hidden Enemy*, by Michael R McDaniel, 29.

we cannot abandon our sons to pornography and masturbation. We cannot desert them to these beasts, these predators.

God placed our sons in our care to train and to protect (Prov. 4:3-4; Eph. 6:4). This requires us to talk to our sons, to prepare our sons for what they will be tempted with. Our Father who is in heaven spoke to us for this reason (Rom. 7:7; Heb. 12:5-13). Solomon wrote the first seven chapters of Proverbs, from which the author of Hebrews was quoting, as a father speaking to his son. He wrote, "Hear, my son, your father's instruction" (Prov. 1:8). One topic that he warns about over and over is sensuality, loose women, and adultery (Prov. 2:16-19; 5:3-20; 6:24-29; 7:5-27). The example is clear. We must talk to our sons plainly, clearly, and often about lust, pornography, and masturbation.

Pornography and Masturbation

Jesus said, "Everyone who looks on a woman to lust for her has committed adultery with her already in his heart" (Matt. 5:28). God had already made it clear, "You shall not commit adultery" (Matt. 5:27).

Some disguise pornography as art, as appreciation for the female form. Some say masturbation is healthy, a safe alternative to sex. It is neither. It is like the honey that drips from the adulteress' lips (Prov. 5:3-5). Pornography and masturbation are bitter in the end.

Pornography and masturbation will destroy a man (Prov. 6:27-28; 7:22-23), ruin a marriage, and steal a man's ability to be intimate. A man's body belongs to his wife (1 Cor. 7:3-4). He has no right to rob his wife of her husband, her marriage, or her husband's intimacy. Even if a man is not yet married his future wife has a right to expect a pure man, a man she can discover sex with in marriage.

If a man shares himself, physically or in heart, with other women what will he have left to give his wife? Solomon said, "Drink water from your own cistern, and fresh water from your own well. Should your springs be dispersed abroad, streams of water in the streets? Let them be yours alone, and not for the stranger with you. Let your fountain be blessed, and rejoice in the wife of your youth" (Prov. 5:15-18).

Pornography and masturbation will build up a wall between a man and his wife. Every secret will add a stone. Each lie will add another. Anger and bitterness will spread like mortar. No woman will be able to satisfy a man in love with pornography and masturbation.

The Solution to Sexual Sin

What can we do if the beast already has hold of us? Can we ever be free? Absolutely! Paul said, "It was for freedom that Christ set us free, therefore keep standing firm and do not be subject again to a yoke of slavery" (Gal. 5:1). Jesus made victory over every sin sure, even over those sins as addictive as pornography and masturbation. Yet, if we do not stand firm, and keep standing firm against them, pornography and masturbation will enslave us.

Jesus expressed this need for constant vigilance best in the garden of Gethsemane. Jesus found His disciples sleeping. They were moments away from Jesus', and their own, greatest trial. Jesus woke them. He told them, "Keep watching and praying, that you may not enter into temptation" (Matt. 26:41).

The devil is always looking for "an opportune time" (Luke 4:13). If we are honest with ourselves we also know when those opportune times are. When we sleep in, but do not sleep. When we stay up late. When we are alone. When we are in front of a computer or behind a magazine rack. We know the temptations are coming, so keep watching.

We will not always be able to foresee the opportunities the devil will exploit. Did David go looking for a bathing woman? No, but there was one. Temptations will find us. It is important therefore, to keep praying. Prayer keeps God's will before our own (Matt. 26:39). Pray, "do not lead us into temptation, but deliver us from evil" (Matt. 6:13). Pray that if temptation must come you will "flee fornication" (1 Cor. 6:18). Pray, and "pray without ceasing" (1 Thess. 5:17).

Conclusion
We likely will never fend off a shark, wrestle an alligator, or climb in a lion filled cage. We will though, as men, face beasts far more dangerous. Therefore, call sin what it is, keep watching, and pray.

Questions
Short Answer
1. What was Cain told to do with sin? _____

_____

2. Where is a man likely to be tempted sexually? _____

_____

3. How does silence help sin? _____

_____

4. What two sins is this lesson about? _____

_____

5. Why must a father talk to his son about sexuality?_____

_____

6. How does Solomon approach the first part of Proverbs?_____

_____

7. What does a bride have the right to expect in her groom? _____

_____

8. What will the sins discussed in the lesson do to a marriage? _____
_____

9. What did Christ set us free from? _____
_____

10. How does watching a praying help us against the sins discussed in this lesson? _____
_____

True of False
_____ 1. Some temptations cannot be resisted.
_____ 2. Sin flourishes when it is done in secret.
_____ 3. Fathers should not talk to their sons about sexuality if either is embarrassed.
_____ 4. A man's body is his own, and he can do with it whatever he wants.
_____ 5. We should pray even when we are not tempted.

Thought Question
Why do you think the words pornography and masturbation, rather than pronouns for each, are repeated so often in this lesson? _____
_____
_____
_____

The Tatooed Lady
Sex, Drugs, and Drink

Once it's on, it's on for good. The tatooed lady did not seem to learn that fact until Jesus, Elvis, and all seven dwarves were nestled among the wrinkles of her back. Needles are not the only things that scar however. Sex, drugs, and drink leave their marks too.

In this lesson I will outline a principle of godliness that addresses all of these. Since now is the time to make up your mind about these, we will discuss this as well.

The Line

There are numerous reasons to avoid each of these vices. Disease, dependence, and death are a few. For this lesson however, I am interested in the reasons the Bible gives.

Start with promiscuous sex. God created and meant for men and women to have and enjoy a sexual life (Gen. 1:28; 2:25; Prov. 5:19; S. of Sol.; 1 Cor. 7:2-3). God placed boundaries on sexuality though (1 Cor. 6:9; Gal. 5:20). The Bible says, "Let marriage be held in honor among all, and let the marriage bed be undefiled; for fornicators and adulterers God will judge" (Heb. 13:4). Sex is wholesome, honorable, and free to be enjoyed by a man and woman who are married to each other. If we are to enjoy it fully however, we must respect these limits.

> Sex is wholesome, honorable, and free to be enjoyed by a man and woman who are married to each other.

Where should daters draw the line then? If only the homerun is foul, is stealing third fair? If a peck on the cheek is sweet, and a kiss on the lips is innocent affection, where else are we permitted to wander?

The same line problem exists for drugs and alcohol. The Bible says, "Do not get drunk with wine" (Eph. 5:18). What about drinking? If alcohol is drunk in moderation is the drinker never drunk? If he is never drunk is his drinking sinless? These questions can only be answered by determining what drunk is. Where is the line that separates drinking from drunkenness? Are we drunk only when the effects, the buzz, are felt? Where does the Bible say that? Are we sober as long as our blood alcohol level is below the state's legal limit? When did man's standard become God's?

For drugs the problem is slightly different. There are no pill poppers, heroin junkies, or potheads, in the Bible, and the only thing smoking is Satan's sulfur pit. Alcohol is a drug though, so the questions asked before would apply here too.

It can be difficult to find, or draw a biblical line on these matters. We still have then the same problem. How far is too far? How much is too much?

The Body is the Temple

There is a principle in the Bible that, if properly understood and honestly applied, will answer these line questions. The apostle Paul wrote, "Do you not know that your body is the temple of the Holy Spirit who dwells in you, whom you have from God, and that you are not your own? For you have been bought with a price: therefore glorify God in your body" (1 Cor. 6:19-20). The Christian's body is God's temple and therefore should be used to glorify rather than dishonor Him (Rom. 2:24).

I do not know what the distance between the first and second base of the dating game is. I do know however, that the hands of a boy and girl snuggling on the sofa under a blanket in a dim lit room are not folded for prayer. The world may not notice a guy at the next table having a beer with his meal, but if he is a known Christian the world will notice.

This is the point that the Proverb writer is making with a series of oddities. He says, "There are three things which are too wonderful for me, four which I do not understand: the way of an eagle in the sky, the way of a serpent on a rock, the way of a ship in the middle of the sea, and the way of a man with a maid. This is the way of an adulterous woman: she eats and wipes her mouth, and says, 'I have done no wrong'" (Prov. 30:18-20). He is asking why does the bird not fall from the sky? How does the snake climb, it has no arms or legs? Why does the ship not sink? Why do boys act so silly around girls? And how can the wicked not see that what they are doing is wicked? How much worse is it when the world can see, but Christians will not!

Does this mean that the world is our standard? If the world sees no difference in shooting heroin and drinking a cup of coffee, does this mean there is no difference? If the world accepts the television evangelist picking up hookers, like a bad boy movie star or musician, does this mean that God accepts both adultery and prostitution? No, of course not. This however, does not negate the point. If the world can see that there is a hog on God's altar, there is a hog on God's altar. How then can Christians join the rebellious rhetoric of Old Testaments Israel saying, "How have we defiled Thee" (Mal. 1:7)?

How Can the Young Secure Their Hearts?

David asked, "How can a young man keep his way pure?" His answer, "By keeping it according to [God's] word" (Ps. 119:9). The Bible tells us what is right, and what is wrong. The Bible also shows how to pursue righteousness and how to avoid evil.

Securing our hearts starts with deciding that we will do what is right, before the test begins. Job said, "I have made a covenant with my eyes; how then could I gaze at a virgin" (Job 31:1). Daniel "made up his mind that he would not defile himself" (Dan. 1:8). Daniel was young. He was far from home. He was in danger, but Daniel's purity was secure because he had already made up his mind to obey God.

Daniel's friends were the same. Did they determine to worship God only after Nebuchadnezzar commanded them to worship his image (Dan. 3:15-18)? What about Peter and John? Did they decide they would preach no matter the cost after they were threatened for preaching (Acts 4:18-20)? Did Joshua choose to serve the Lord only after he knew whom everyone else was going to serve (Josh. 24:15)? No. They all determined to do what was right before they were tested.

The apostle Paul wrote, "Finally, be strong in the Lord, and in the strength of His might. Put on the full armor of God, that you may be able to stand firm against the schemes of the devil" (Eph. 6:10-11). What warrior waits, until the battle is raging, to put his armor on? The soldier puts his armor on before going to battle. The man of God does too, so when the battle begins he can, "stand firm . . . having *already* gird [his] loins with truth, and having *already* put on the breastplate of righteousness" (Eph. 6:14-17).

Choosing to do what is right is the first step, but this must be followed up with deeds. You must put the armor to use. You must "prove yourselves doers of the word" and not deluded soldier impersonators (James 1:22). These are the guys who buy the gear at the surplus store, march around in the fatigues, but never get them dirty.

Conclusion

Remember, once it's on, it's on for good. Though the sins of sex, drugs, and drink can be forgiven the scars they leave can be deep, painful, and lifelong.

Questions

Short Answer

1. What are some reasons to avoid sex, drugs, and alcohol? _____
   _____
2. What boundaries does God place on sex? _____
   _____
3. Why are the feelings of intoxication not a good line for determining drunkenness? _____
   _____
4. Since our bodies are the temple of God, how should they be used? _____
   _____
5. What can the Proverb writer not understand about the way of an adulterous woman? _____
   _____
6. What does the world think of Christians who drink, smoke, and visit a make-out point? _____
   _____
7. Why did Israel ask, "How have we defiled Thee"? _____
   _____
8. How can the young secure their hearts? _____
   _____
9. Where was Daniel when he was tested? _____
   _____
10. What enables a soldier to stand firm during the battle? _____
    _____

True or False

_____ 1. God created sex for a husband and his wife to enjoy.
_____ 2. People are not drunk until they reach the state's legal limit.
_____ 3. Difficulty in drawing a line means no line can be drawn.
_____ 4. There is no difference in shooting heroin and drinking a cup of coffee.
_____ 5. We do not need to think about how we will act until we are on a date, offered a beer, or given a cigarette.

Thought Question

What other areas of life will the fact that a Christian is to glorify God in their body affect? _____
_____
_____
_____

Worth The Admission
Being A Mate Worth Choosing

Whether we have tickets to the circus, the movies, or a game, the big man does too. The big man is the sports fan who goes to the game in a painted on shirt. He wears the foam fingers and hat, and throughout the game he never sits down. It would not matter if he did though, because that hat would still be in the way. While our backside goes numb, the big man's backside is all we have to stare at. We then wonder, is this worth the admission?

Forsaking all others is a big price tag, but it is the price that you wear. It is the marriage admission. Are you worth it? In this lesson we will discuss being worth someone's choosing, being a mate worth the admission.

Becoming Mister Right

The divorce rate is up. The divorce rate is down. Whichever it is, the fact stands that there are a lot of divorces. There are a lot of people who do not think their spouse and marriage are worth the admission. There are even more who, though they are still married, feel the same.

Part of the problem in marriage, as with dating, is that we spend most of the time looking for the right significant other. I want a girl who is happy, who smiles, who sweetens ice tea with a touch. Oh yeah, and I want her to like me even though I'm a selfish sour cynic. Why would Miss Right want Mister Wrong? The fact is she doesn't. So what effort will you put in to making yourself Mister Right?

As in the lesson on friendship, I am not suggesting that we pretend to be someone we are not. If we have blemishes on our character however, I am suggesting that we use some oxy-clear. James says this is how the Bible ought to be read, with an eye and intent to clean up our inward man. He wrote, "Therefore putting aside all filthiness and all that remains of wickedness, in humility receive the word implanted, which is able to save your souls. But prove your-

selves doers of the word" (James 1:21-22). Paul made the same point when he wrote, "lay aside the old self . . . and put on the new" (Eph. 4:22-24).

This character clear up is what this book is about too. Miss Right wants a self-respecting man who knows manliness is honorable. Miss Right wants a man who is a Christian and who will help her reach heaven. Miss Right wants a man who knows how to treat other people, a man who controls his emotions, his tongue, and his urges. Miss Right wants a man who will work, who will lead, and who will make the most of what he has. Miss Right wants Mister Right.

Job is a biblical embodiment of this well-groomed man, this Mister Right. Job 31 describes the worthy man, just as Proverbs 31 describes the worthy woman. Job begins with loyalty. The worthy man is loyal to his wife, even with his eyes (Job 31:1). The worthy man is honest in everything he does (Job 31:5-6). The worthy man is fair even to his critics (Job 31:13-15). The worthy man is gener-ous (Job 31:16-19), he trusts in God and not wealth (Job 31:24-28), and is a friend even to his enemies (Job 31:29-32).

> . . . there are a lot of people who will not share the values that you as a godly man have, values that you will want in a girl. This can make finding a date, and more so finding a wife, difficult.

Loneliness

You may ask, "What happens though, if Miss Right and I cannot find each other?" First, do not interpret my use of Miss Right to mean that there is just one right person in the whole world for you. This is not so. For one reason, God has never told us to marry the person we love, but rather to love the person we marry (Eph. 5:25, 28; Tit. 2:4). Whoever we are married to then, we can love, just as Hosea loved his unfaithful wife Gomer (Hos. 3:1). Like Gomer though, the daughter of her society, there are a lot of people who will not share the values that you as a godly man have, values that you will want in a girl. This can make finding a date, and more so finding a wife, difficult.

Again, some may wonder, "What do I do when my friends are all getting married, and I cannot even find a date to take to their wedding?" What happens when loneliness moves in like a freeloading roommate?

First, do not settle. There are worse things than being lonely. Being lonely in a marriage is one.

Couples of course will settle on some things. She is a Crest girl. He is a Colgate guy. They settle on being an Aim family. Surrendering your brand of toothpaste however, is not like giving up Christ and His church. Keep in mind that while Hosea loved Gomer his love did not keep that worldly woman from making his life and marriage miserable. Marrying a daughter of our society will not be any better.

Second, get involved in doing things for other people. Loneliness can be a sort of self-fulfilling state. We can become so focused on how lonely we are, I am, me, that we quit thinking about others. They in turn quit thinking about us. We push others away so we have more room to wallow in our how-lonely-I-am sty, and then surprise—no one wants to get down in the mud hole with us.

When Elijah hid in the cave from Jezebel he told God, "I alone am left" (1 Kings 19:10). This was not true from God's greater perspective (1 Kings 19:18). Still, there is no doubt that the prophet felt, right then, very lonely. He had however, only days before, left his servant in Beersheba and went on alone (1 Kings 19:3). Elijah did therefore, bring a measure of loneliness on himself, but God lets that point go. What God does however, is interesting.

God first asked Elijah, "What are you doing here" (1 Kings 19:9). Do you think the question was for God's benefit, God did not know? No it was to get Elijah thinking, thinking most of all about what he was doing or maybe not doing. After God asks the question again He gives Elijah something to do. He is to go and anoint a new king over Aram and another over Israel. He is then to anoint Elisha to take his place (1 Kings 19:15-16).

We will all face times of loneliness, even those as strong as Elijah. When we are lonely though we need to ask ourselves, "What am I doing?" Then we need to get busy.

Dating

In the Bible marriages were arranged. The Father of us all arranged the marriage of Adam and Eve (Gen. 2:22). Abraham made arrangements to find Isaac

a wife (Gen. 24:1-4). In parts of the world parents still arrange marriages for their children, but this is not how it works in America.

You will choose a wife from the girls you date. However, since dating did not exist in Bible times there are no direct biblical instructions for dating. There

Boy It's a Circus

are however, principles to consider.[1]

First, not so much a biblical principle as one man's observation, having seen both sides of the wedding, dating is not marriage and marriage is not dating. They are no more the same than babysitting is parenting, and it is better to learn this on the dating side.

Second, be careful with feelings. I know the reality is we get hurt, and we hurt others. We do not mean to of course, but we like some girl and she just wants to be friends. Another girl likes us, and well, we barrow the first girl's friendship idea. We get hurt, and we hurt others. While this may be reality still, be careful. Girls have feelings too. They want to be liked. They fear rejection and embarrassment just as you and I do. So again be careful. Remember the Lord's command, "however you want people to treat you, so treat them" (Matt. 7:12).

Finally, enjoy this time. Solomon wrote, "Rejoice, young man, during your childhood, and let your heart be pleasant during the days of young manhood" (Eccl. 11:9). There is a lot of craziness wrapped up in being a teenager. Boy, it's a circus sometimes, but the time is fleeting. This time does not last forever (Eccl. 9:10). I thought my freshmen year would never end, but it did, my senior year too. My first house, where the young people from church hung out after services, ate pizza, and played cards is gone, buried under a carwash. The truck I bought in high school belongs to someone else now. I kissed a girl for the first time in that pick-up. It was early August. It was early evening. And I was twenty-two.

I am not twenty-two anymore. It is late summer now and the foliage is beginning to thin. The limbs groan some too when bent. Still, autumn is a good time. It is the time acorns are planted.

I am not ashamed of my past, and I do not want you to be ashamed of yours. Yes, there are things I wish I had done. Some things I wish I would have done differently. Still, I can reminisce with a smile, and hope that those who knew me then can too. I want to finish with the warning that Solomon gives. Enjoy your youth but do not sour the memories by doing things you will be ashamed of later because, "God will bring you to judgment for all these things" (Eccl. 9:9).

Conclusion

Miss Right is looking for Mister Right. When she meets you will she have found him? Forsaking all others is a high price for just any man, but it is a bargain for the one worth the admission.

---

[1] Gonn and Hal Iggulden have a pithy section about girls and dating in their book, *The Dangerous Book for Boys.*

Questions
Short Answer
1. What is the price or admission for marriage? _____

_____

2. What should be done with character blemishes? _____

_____

3. What should be our purpose in reading the Bible? _____

_____

4. What are the qualities of a worthy man? _____

_____

5. How was Gomer the daughter of her society? _____

_____

6. What do you think "settling" means in reference to dating and marriage? __

_____

7. What did Elijah do with his servant? _____

_____

8. When Elijah was lonely what did God ask him, and why is the question significant? _____

_____

9. If feelings are still going to be hurt why should we be careful? _____

_____

10. Solomon tells us to enjoy our youth, but what two warnings does he give? _

_____

True or False
_____ 1. Ms. Right is looking for Mr. Wrong.
_____ 2. There is only one right person for us.
_____ 3. Strong people like Elijah are sometimes lonely.
_____ 4. The Bible can give no guidance on the matter of dating.
_____ 5. We should enjoy the time we have.

Thought Question
Why do you think this lesson on being a mate worth choosing comes before the lesson on choosing a mate?

_____

_____

_____

_____

A Bear in a Bonnet
How to Choose a Wife

Have you ever seen trained bears? Their handlers dress them in costumes and have them perform for the audience. They seem so sweet and gentle, as much as the stuffed animals children cuddle with for comfort, but one fact must never be forgotten. It does not matter how a bear is dressed. A bear is still a bear, with bear teeth and bear claws.

Girls can be this way too. It does not matter what she looks like, sounds like, or smells like. It does not matter how she dresses. A bear of a woman will be a bear to live with.

God said, however, "It is not good for the man to be alone; I will make him a helper suitable for him" (Gen. 2:18). In this lesson we will consider what God solved Adam's problem with. This will help us determine what kind of girl will be a good girl friend and later a good wife.

Homosexuality

God made Eve for Adam (Gen. 2:22). God made a woman for the man, and the man married her. Abraham, Isaac, and Jacob all married women (Gen. 11:29; 24:67; 29:28). Joseph, David, and Peter likewise, all married women (Gen. 41:45; 1 Sam. 18:27; Mark 1:30). Not a single man of godly character was a homosexual.

Someone tempted with homosexual desires may respond, "I was born this way." If this were the case would it make homosexuality right? Would it reverse what the Bible says about it? No. God destroyed the Sodomites because they practiced homosexuality (Gen. 19:4-5, 24-25). Whether any was born with a homosexual desire did not matter. What mattered was what they did. Paul called homosexuality an "indecent act," "error" (Rom. 1:27), and "unrighteous" (1 Cor. 6:9). Paul said, those who practiced homosexuality were, "sinners . . . unholy . . . and profane" (1 Tim. 1:9-10).

Why does it not matter whether a person is born with homosexual desires? It does not matter because temptation is not sin. Sinning is sin (James 1:13-15). An alcoholic is a sinner, not because his father was an alcoholic and because there is a genetic link in alcoholism, but because he himself drinks alcohol. A fornicator is a sinner, not because he wants to have sex with women as God designed him, but because he has sex with women he is not married to. A homosexual is a sinner not because he is temped to have sex with men, whether he was born with such desires or not, but because he acts on those desires. He is a homosexual because he engages in homosexuality.

Again, it would not matter if it could be proved that homosexuality is genetic, *natural* for some people, because God calls us to control our desires, to deny ourselves (Luke 9:23). When Jesus was hungry, a natural desire, He was tempted to satisfy His desire in a godless way (Matt. 4:2-4). Jesus refused. Jesus controlled His hunger. Jesus controlled His nature. Even if homosexual desires could be proved natural, God's word would not change.

Attractiveness

God made a woman for Adam, but was she pretty? "Isn't it important to be attracted to the girl?" Boys ask this question, sincere boys, good boys, boys who want to please God, and yet are still boys. Men and boys look at the world through the eyes of men. They live within the bodies of men, and they deserve an answer that does not belittle them for being, or expressing what men are, men with feelings and desires given to them by God.

God did not fashion woman as she is by accident. It is therefore, neither shallow nor evil to appreciate a girl for her looks. Sarai, Abram's wife, was "a beautiful woman" (Gen. 12:11). Rachel was more attractive than her sister Leah (Gen. 29:17). Samson too married a girl because, "she look[ed] good to [him]" (Judg. 14:3). In each case however, the woman's beauty brings heartache to her husband. Does this mean only unattractive girls make good wives? No. What this means is that sadness and suffering follow where physical beauty is the most important or only condition.

While God gave us a body with eyes that enjoy beauty, God also placed within our bodies a brain, and expects us to control the rest of our body with it.

Paul wrote, "I want women to adorn themselves with proper clothing, modestly and discreetly, not with braided hair and gold or pearls or costly garments; but rather by means of good works, as befits women making a claim to godliness" (2 Tim. 2:9-10). While these instructions are to women, there is an important implication here for men too.

Since Paul's comments are to promote modesty it is evident that women maybe tempted to dress immodestly. Why? Why are some women tempted to dress this way? Whether the outfit is too high on the lower end, too low on the upper end, too tight at every end, or with the ends minus the middle, the purpose is the same: to draw the attention of men to the woman's body.

In Paul's statement he does not forbid women from wearing jewelry any more than he forbids them from wearing garments. Paul however, is directing women to place greater importance on "good works," than on how they "adorn" themselves outwardly. The implication to men is the same. Of course, men should dress modestly too, but men should place more importance on what a woman does than what she looks like.

Women who dress modestly help men avoid temptations of lust. In the same way men will aid women in resisting temptations to dress provocatively by desiring a "claim to godliness" more than a pretty face and firm figure.

Man's Helper
Helpmeet was not her name. Her name was Eve, but she was man's helper. She aided him in fulfilling God's commands. God said, "be fruitful and multiply, and fill the earth" (Gen. 1:28). How would Adam have done this without Eve? Again God said, "cultivate [the garden] and keep it" (Gen. 2:15). A lazy or self-serving woman could not have helped Adam.

But the most important aspect of her helping nature is revealed in the next command. "And the Lord God commanded the man saying, 'From any tree of the garden you may eat freely; but from the tree of the knowledge of good and evil you shall not eat'" (Gen. 2:16-17). A woman is her husband's spiritual helper. Eve influenced Adam's spirituality, but not for good; she did bring the forbidden fruit to Adam. But the impact that women have in their husband's spiritual life, for good or bad, is clear and profound.

One question that often comes up is, "Can a Christian marry a non-Christian?" If not, what about dating a non-Christian, where emotional attachments begin? There are examples of Christians being married to non-Christians in the Bible. It is impossible to determine whether this mix existed before they married, or if one obeyed the gospel after the wedding? As it is today, both situations were probably found in ancient days. None of these however, was commanded to separate from his unbelieving spouse (1 Cor. 7:12-13).

What does this prove? Does *can* matter as much as *should*? Is it wise? A man's wife will have a tremendous influence on his spirituality. If she is in rebellion to the Lord she will tempt her husband to rebel too. If she is a Christian but a lukewarm Christian she will make her husband tepid. If however, she is zealous for the Lord as her husband is then they will help one another. As the proverb states, "Iron sharpens iron, so one man sharpens another" (Prov. 27:17). It is not enough to date and marry a church member. Marry someone who will help you get to heaven. Marry someone who is a faithful follower of Jesus Christ.

Conclusion

God made woman. He made her attractive and to be man's helper. A woman like this will be a "gift from the Lord" (Prov. 19:14) to any man, but a bear of a woman will be a bear to live with.

Questions
Short Answer

1. Why did God destroy the Sodomites? _____

_____

2. How does Paul describe homosexuality? _____

_____

3. What makes a person an alcoholic, a fornicator, or a homosexual? _____

_____

4. What happens to those who treat physical beauty as the most important feature? _____

_____

5. Why are women tempted to dress immodestly? _____

_____

6. What implication does Paul's command to women, that they dress modestly, have on men? _____

_____

7. What was Eve supposed to help Adam do? _____

_____

8. How did Eve influence Adam's spiritual life? _____

_____

9. What question is better than, can a Christian marry a non-Christian? _____

_____

10. A man who is going to heaven will want what kind of helper? _____

_____

True or False

_____ 1. A homosexual is a person who practices homosexuality.

_____ 2. It is wrong to like girls who are pretty.

Boy It's a Circus

_____ 3. The most attractive people are the happiest people.
_____ 4. The woman we marry can either help us or hinder us from going to heaven.
_____ 5. It is enough to marry a church member.

Thought Question
What qualities do you want in a girl friend, and later a wife? _____
_____
_____
_____
_____
_____

In the Spotlight
Leadership

Fame. Importance. The spotlight. A leader may have all of these, but a leader does not cling to any of them. The ringmaster is important. He stands in the spotlight. He may even be famous, but the ringmaster is not the show. The ringmaster simply introduces the show and moves the spotlight on.

In this chapter we will explore some aspects of the leadership stage: who has the job of leading, how to do a good job as a leader, and when to start preparing for our own time in the spotlight.

In the Home and in the Church

God made the husband, leader of the home. The apostle Paul wrote, "the husband is the head of the wife, as Christ also is head of the church" (Eph. 5:23). Just as the head controls the body, the husband leads the wife. He will make decisions that answer questions like, who's name will we use? Where will we live? How will we spend money?

Someone will say this isn't fair. Worse, someone may say, this is chauvinistic dinosaurism. What church member though, would say to Jesus, "How dare you tell me to wear the name Christian. Who crowned you king? It's not fair for you to tell me what kind of worship to offer, what kind of music to worship with, or how to eat the Lord's Supper." Christ is head of the church, so Christ has made these decisions, just as the husband will make decisions in the home.

Now a wise husband will want to know what his wife thinks about various matters. He will never use his authority simply to please himself, because the verse on headship continues, "as Christ also is the head of the church, He Himself being the Savior of the body" (Eph. 5:23). Jesus saved the church by dying and pouring out His blood. This was not what He wanted to do (Matt. 26:39). The disciples, who would soon be the church, even thought it was the wrong

decision (Matt. 16:21-22). Still, Jesus died because His blood was what the church needed. Likewise a wise husband will be selfless, considering his wife, but still he will make the decisions in his home.

In the local church, men are also to lead. Paul said, "I want the men in every place to pray . . . but I do not allow a woman to teach or exercise authority over a man" (1 Tim. 2:8, 12). Concerning the specific work of elders Paul wrote, "If any man aspires to the work of overseer, it is a fine work he desires to do" (1 Tim. 3:1). The first qualification for an elder is that he be a man. Those who lead the church in study, song, and prayer also need to be men.

The warning given to husbands before is also given to elders here. The apostle Peter wrote to elders saying, "shepherd the flock of God among you, exercising oversight. . . not yet as lording it over those allotted to your charge" (1 Pet. 5:2-3). Elders are to do something. They are to exercise oversight. Elders will make decisions about who will do the preaching, and when to withdraw from an unfaithful brother or sister. They will also make financial decisions. Peter clarifies that this work, this authority, is not that of lord, or boss. It is not ordering people to jump, and expecting a "How high, sir" response, just because you can. The eldership is a work of service. It is "proving to be examples to the flock" (1 Pet. 5:3). It is caring first for the flock, not the shepherd.

Descriptions of a Good Leader

While God has made husbands and elders the leaders, God also expects them to be good leaders, not title-holders. Following are a few suggestions on being a good leader.

A good leader leads from the front. A good general may not always or ever be on the front lines with his men, but he does not demand his men do what he himself would refuse to do. Jesus led His disciples to serve one another by serving them. He had the right to demand that they serve one another because of His position. He was Jesus. He was the Son of God. He was and is the King of Kings. All things had been given into his hands (John 13:3). He was greater than His servants, but He did not refuse to do what He commanded His servants to do. Jesus bent down and did the job of a servant. He washed the disciples' feet, and then commanded that they serve one another.

A good leader cares for those he leads. The shepherd and the hired man both lead sheep, but the difference between the two is evident when danger threatens. The shepherd cares for the sheep. He protects them even with his own life. The hireling sacrifices the sheep to save himself. Jesus cares, and demonstrates that He is "the good shepherd" because He "lays down His life for the sheep" (John 10:11).

When Jesus invites people to, "Come to Me, all who are weary and heavy-laden, and I will give you rest. Take My yoke upon you, and learn from Me, for I am gentle and humble in heart; and you shall find rest for your souls. For My yoke is easy, and My load is light" (Matt. 11:28-30), His invitation is somewhat ironic. Jesus gives them rest by giving them work to do. Jesus however, is gentle. He cares for His own, and that is why they have rest even though they have work to do.

A good contrast is Boxer in George Orwell's classic *Animal Farm*. Boxer the great workhorse exhausts himself working the farm, and when his strength is used up he is sold to the glue factory. Jesus will not discard His people after we have given Him our best. He will not use us up and then throw us away. Jesus is the good shepherd. Jesus is the best leader.

A good leader is humble too. A good leader is willing to let another go first. He is willing to let others be important. Jesus exhibited this humility of mind, when He, "emptied Himself, taking the form of a bond-servant" (Phil. 2:7). Jesus did not grasp or cling to His glorious form or His highly exalted position. Jesus let these go because He considered our interests and needs as more important.

Good leaders are not the loudest people in the room. Good leaders are not always the people in charge. Good leaders are those people who care about what is best, whether it is best for themselves or not, and then guide people through the opportunities they have in that good direction.

Preparing For Leadership

Starting early is key to being ready. Just like saving for retirement. It is too late to start saving at age sixty-four if you plan to retire at age sixty-five. You need to start preparing in your twenties. Whether in the home or the eldership, preparation needs to start before we are old enough to serve.

Three of the qualifications for elders can illustrate how we can start preparing early. Paul wrote that an elder must be, "respectable, hospitable, able to teach" (1 Tim. 3:2).

Can a teen be respectable? Can he be hospitable? Can he be able to teach? Certainly. Since being respectable means to behave anyone tempted to misbehave can resist and demonstrate a respectable spirit.

Again, if we think of hospitality in simple terms like friendliness, the attitude that hospitality stems from, we can all be hospitable. We may not be able to have people over to our house, but what about God's house. Can a teenager invite people to worship? When visitors comes can a teen greet them? Can he make the visitor feel welcome?

The last of the three, being able to teach, begins with being willing to learn. Making time to study the Bible class lesson and participate in class lays the foundation for teaching later.

Conclusion

As husbands, as elders, as men we will lead. But leader is not a title. It is a work. It is a work done best when the leader thinks first about those who come after.

Questions
Short Answer

1. Who is the head of the home? _____

2. Why did Christ sacrifice Himself to save the church? _____
_____

3. What role do men serve in the church? _____
_____

4. What kinds of decisions will elders make? _____
_____

5. What does "lording it" mean? _____
_____

6. How did Jesus lead His disciples to serve one another? _____
_____

7. How is the shepherd different from the hired man? _____
_____

8. What did Jesus do that showed He was a humble leader? _____
_____

9. When should men start preparing to serve as elders? _____
_____

10. What are some ways to be hospitable? _____
_____

True or False

_____ 1. A leader will only make decisions that others agree with.

_____ 2. Jesus saved the church by doing what He wanted.

_____ 3. Being willing to let others have the spotlight is a characteristic of a good leader.

_____ 4. The best leader is always the most outspoken person.

_____ 5. Being willing to learn now is the foundation for being able to teach later.

Thought Question

Making decisions that people do not like is the test of a leader. In these situations how can a leader balance being bossy and being indecisive? _____
_____
_____
_____

Big Top or Little Tent
Making the Most of What You Have

Thirty elephants, a dozen tigers, and an army of acrobats do not make a circus great. Two five-year-olds put on a show that, in my estimation, rivaled any Ringling Brothers production, not for flash but for joy of watching. One was the master of ceremonies and the other a clown. One was the tamer and the other a lion. One walked a rope laid along the floor and the other gasped in suspense. They did all of this under the big top—some bed sheets thrown over the kitchen chairs.

In this last lesson I want to help you be happy with who you are. I want to help you be content with uncontrollable circumstances. I want to help you not be bogged down with feeling of inferiority.

Our circumstances in this life are all different. But each can live a happy and successful life if he views his life from heaven's vantage.

Life is Not Fair

We live in a world where bad things happen. Bad things happen to good people, to innocent people.

One reason for this is that people sometimes act in ways that hurt other people. For every Abel there is a Cain (Gen. 4:8). For every abused, teased, or picked on person there is some bully. For every victim of a drunk driver there is someone driving drunk.

Sometimes however, bad things happen with no one to blame. People live with birth defects, poverty, and debilitating illnesses. Did someone sin that caused these things to be (John 9:1-3)? No, but we live in an imperfect world where thorns and thistles grow (Gen. 3:18).

The fact is life is not always fair. Joseph's brothers sold him into slavery (Gen. 37:18-33). His master's wife lied about him, and Joseph was jailed (Gen. 39:7-20). Lazarus was a beggar (Luke 16:20-22). He was crippled likely, with bedsores, and dog spit was his only medicine. Lazarus was a broken, friendless man. I think it is fair to conclude that he died this way. Job was robbed of every good thing, his wealth, and his family. He was robbed of his physical health, and his reputation (Job 1:13-19; 2:7; 30:1-10). Countless descendants were promised to

Abraham, but in his lifetime he had only one.[1] His brother however, had twelve (Gen. 22:20-24). Peter was jailed (Acts 4:3). Stephen was stoned (Acts 7:58-60). Jesus was crucified (John 19:17-19).

Life will not always be fair to you. It has not always been fair to me. Arguing about who has the worst hard-luck story however, is beside the point. What we need to take from these thorny facts is that we can overcome them, grow from them, and become stronger or spiritually mature.

Strength from Struggle

It's true; struggles make us stronger. James says, "Consider it all joy, my brethren, when you encounter various trials, knowing that the testing of your faith produces endurance" (James 1:2-3). If exercising and testing our muscles makes them physically stronger then exercising our spiritual muscle, our faith, will make us spiritually stronger or mature. After giving us this theme James fills his letter with examples of these various trials or spiritual exercises. The first is the search for wisdom (James 1:5-8). Accepting God's wisdom is difficult especially when the world's experts preach a different wisdom, but looking to God for answers will make us stronger.

> **Living is not about being paid more, dating a cuter girl, or being remembered longer after you retire.**

The letter of James is not the only place we find this principle that strength comes from struggle. The author of Hebrews tells us that even Jesus, "learned obedience from the things which He suffered" (Heb. 5:8). Paul's thorn in the flesh testified that God's grace was sufficient for him (2 Cor. 12:9).

The story of Joseph is a good example of this too. When Moses, the author of Genesis, introduces Joseph he is the favored son of Jacob. Joseph also seems to gloat about the position. He tells his brothers about a dream he had. His brothers' sheaves of grain gathered around and bowed down before his own, indicating that he was to rule over them (Gen. 37:6-11).

As a sign of this favoritism Jacob, the father, gives Joseph a special coat of many colors (Gen. 37:3). Joseph receives two more coats before his story ends, and it is these coats that are particularly interesting to the development of Joseph.[2]

---

[1] While Abraham had other children such as Ishmael the promise was to be fulfilled through Sarah (Gen. 17:18-19).

[2] These thoughts on Joseph's coats are barrowed with great appreciation from Steve Wolfgang.

Joseph's brothers take this first coat and use it to deceive their father, making him think Joseph is dead while they sell Joseph into slavery (Gen. 37:30-33). His exalted position vanishes in a day. Eventually however, Joseph is sold to Potiphar in Egypt. While in Potiphar's house God blesses his work, and Potiphar favors Joseph, putting him in charge. When Patiphar's wife however, tries to seduce him Joseph runs from the house and leaves his coat. Potiphar's wife uses Joseph's coat, just as his brothers had, to lie about him. Joseph again finds himself in the pit (Gen. 39:1-20). In time Joseph is lifted from prison and interprets the Pharaoh's dream. Pharaoh places Joseph in charge of all Egypt. Only in the throne was the Pharaoh greater. In this favored position, Pharaoh gives Joseph another new coat (Gen. 41:42). When his brothers then come and bow before Joseph, as he had predicted in his youth, he does not gloat, or take revenge. Joseph is merciful. I wonder, if Joseph had not worn the first two coats and suffered as he had, could he have worn the last coat and worn it with honor, or would the power have made him conceited?

The author of Hebrews makes the point well. He says, "All discipline for the moment seems not to be joyful, but sorrowful; yet to those who have been trained by it, afterwards it yields the peaceful fruits of righteousness" (Heb. 12:11).

Of Winners and Losers
There is one last point. If life is not fair how can we determine who the winners are? How can we know who is the best, who is first?

While competition has a place in life, the act of living should not be summed up in points, accumulating more points than your neighbor. Living is not about being paid more, dating a cuter girl, or being remembered longer after you retire. If these were the categories that determine the value of a person's life what would we have to say about Lazarus, Jesus, Peter, or Paul? Were their lives failures?

Living is about pleasing God. The apostle Paul said, "we have as our ambition, whether at home or absent, to be pleasing to Him" (2 Cor. 5:9). When Paul wrote to the Philippians he said, "For to me, to live is Christ" (Phil. 1:21). That is a powerful and concise summary on living, but it is magnified when considered in the context of the whole letter to the Philippians.

Paul tells the Philippians about his time in prison (Phil. 1:12-14). He is separated from the Philippians, his friends, and does not have the freedom to go visit them. His attitude, however, is "my circumstances have turned out for the greater progress of he gospel" (Phil. 1:12). Paul tells about ambitious preachers, out making a name for themselves, who seem to think that Paul will be jealous of their success (Phil. 1:15-17). Paul's attitude again is, "Christ is proclaimed; and in this I rejoice" (Phil. 1:18). Paul explains that this was the attitude that Jesus had (Phil. 2:5-11). Jesus gave up His exalted form or position and took the form or position of a servant, and he did so to serve us.

It is with this view that success can be judged. It does not matter where I am. It does not matter with whom I am or from whom I am separated. It does not matter what I have or what I do not have. If I am serving the Lord then "I can do all things" (Phil. 4:13).

Conclusion

I want to conclude this book with these thoughts. Our big top may be a small tent, but if a small tent is all we have then set it up and use it to serve the Lord.

Questions
Short Answer

1. Why do bad things sometimes happen to good people? _____
   _____

2. How was life unfair to Joseph? _____
   _____

3. What other Bible characters faced difficulties in life?_____
   _____

4. What will struggles and difficulties do for us? _____
   _____

5. What did Jesus learn from His suffering?_____
   _____

6. What did Paul's thorn in the flesh teach him? _____
   _____

7. How did Joseph's trials change him? _____
   _____

8. When Paul said, "for to me, to live is Christ" (Phil. 1:21), what was he saying about life and living? _____
   _____
   _____

9. Even though Paul was imprisoned what was he happy about? _____
   _____

10. How is success in life to be judged? _____
    _____

True or False

_____ 1. Bad things happen to people sometimes through no fault of their own.
_____ 2. Spiritual strength comes from spiritual challenges just as physical strength develops from physical exercises.
_____ 3. All discipline for the moment seems joyful (Heb. 12:11).

_____ 4. Lazarus, Jesus, Peter, and Paul were all failures.

_____ 5. No matter what we have we ought to use it to serve the Lord.

Thought Question

What are the things Paul is talking about when he says, "I can do all things" (Phil. 4:13)? _____

_____

_____

_____

www.ingramcontent.com/pod-product-compliance
Lightning Source LLC
Chambersburg PA
CBHW032029040426
42448CB00006B/787